S0-FMM-729

RURAL PARISH!

Rural Parish!

A Year from the Journal of

ANNA LAURA GEBHARD

ILLUSTRATED BY
JANET SMALLEY

ABINGDON-COKESBURY PRESS
New York • *Nashville*

RURAL PARISH!

COPYRIGHT, MCMXLVII
BY STONE & PIERCE

All rights in this book are reserved. No part of the
text may be reproduced in any form without written permission of the publishers, except brief quotations used
in connection with reviews in magazines or newspapers.

B

Scripture quotations designated "Moffatt" are
from *The Bible: A New Translation* by James
Moffatt, copyright 1935 by Harper & Brothers.

SET UP, PRINTED, AND BOUND BY THE
PARTHENON PRESS AT NASHVILLE, TEN-
NESSEE, UNITED STATES OF AMERICA

Contents

I

EARLY WINTER 9

II

LATE WINTER 41

III

SPRING 61

IV

SUMMER 80

V

AUTUMN 103

PART I

EARLY WINTER

Stand still, think of the wonders of God.
   When God works, do you know how? . . .
Have you ever roused the morning,
   given directions to the dawn? . . .
Have you ever entered the stores of the snow?
   Have you seen the arsenals of hail—
the hail I keep for stormy days,
   for battery and assault?
How are the mists marshalled,
   that scatter fresh water on earth? . . .
Who taught the feathery clouds,
   or trained the meteors?
Who has the skill to mass the clouds,
   or tilt the pitchers of the sky?
                —From Job 37 and 38 (Moffatt)

FRIDAY, OCTOBER 15

"And here, Laurie, is our church."

Our car came to a stop. With eager anticipation I looked out at the one-room building before us. I could think only of a little stray white dog at a deserted intersection. I looked back into Ed's warm eyes, trying to hide the chill of misgiving I felt.

"I warned you not to expect too much," he said. "After all, its the people not the building we're here to serve."

"I know, Ed. And we asked for a rural parish, didn't we? We wanted to serve the places others might pass by."

9

"Well, I guess we're here. Let's go in."

We crossed the dirt path to the chipped concrete steps. We opened the ill-fitting door and stepped into the empty room. In the rear stood an old wood stove, an immense jacket around it. My eyes followed the straight black stovepipe the full length of the room to the front of the church. There underneath the chimney hole was a simple altar, adorned by a white wood cross and two candlesticks, with a backdrop of purple velvet. It was the one touch of beauty in the entire barren room. The pulpit stood on one side, the chairs for the choir on the other. On either side of the bare aisle the pews were lined up in perfect order. They were like the road to heaven—straight and narrow.

I looked out of the narrow arched windows with their drab gray frames and noticed two boys playing marbles in the dusty sand of the street. An ancient car honked at them, and as they moved slowly out of the way, it chugged by.

"It may not be so grand as what we've been seeing on our honeymoon, but it's remarkable what it becomes when the pews are full of people," Ed assured me. I looked up at him, and his eyes twinkled. "Anyway, Laurie, take heart. Gorman is just one of our churches. We've a couple of others, you know. You'll like the neat white building at the Fairhaven crossroads."

"And Gold Valley?"

"Well, it's like the town—sorta run down and discouraged."

"Your bride has a lot to learn. It's going to seem strange, living here at Gorman but belonging to three communities."

"Just wait till you ride the circuit for a while," Ed told me. "It's like a merry-go-round—Wednesday, Gorman; Thursday, Fairhaven; and Friday, Gold Valley."

10

"And Sundays, all three. Well, at least we won't carry all our eggs in one basket!"

MONDAY, OCTOBER 18

Tonight at sunset we wandered back to the garden plot behind the parsonage. Gardens in October are like old

men—they have borne their best fruits and are full of memories. Just beyond the barn our neighbors were gathering in their gladiola and dahlia bulbs.

"Say, Reverend," called out old Mr. Gunter, "come on over. Ever grow dahlias? Got a Lady Lavender here that took the county fair. And my Jersey Reds were big as dinner plates. Wish you could've seen 'em. I'll split the bulbs come spring, and we'll plant some between the gardens."

We picked our way across the garden stubble, past their patch of pumpkins, large and orange against the gray soil, to the glad and dahlia bed. The rosy haze of the sunset

11

flooded the Gunters' kindly old faces. How like the setting of the sun their own lives seemed!

"Look at them colors!" Mr. Gunter exclaimed, lifting his face to the sky. "Why, even our plain little church looks perty agin that sky." And it did.

"Yep," he added reflectively, "me and Fannie been livin' close to that church a long time. It means plenty to us, son. Gorman ain't exactly a friendly town. And that little church is like—well, it's like an island in rough waters. Remember that, son."

THURSDAY, OCTOBER 21

"Now you folks come on out an' see us," Farmer Stanton admonished after the Fairhaven service last Sunday. "Course 'tain't so easy to find our place, but when ye git there, ye'll find a welcome that'll bring you back agin."

Today we found that welcome. We drove north across the Gorman plain to the rolling hills around Fairhaven crossroads that shelter a hundred sky-filled lakes and hold rolling fields with fringes of wilderness upon their backs. The haze of late autumn was upon the hills today, and only here and there among the trees were tattered remnants of the golds and russets of fall.

Ed found Farmer Stanton plowing the west forty, and I found Mrs. Stanton in the neat farm kitchen, lifting hot loaves of bread from the oven.

"You folks jes' go on in," Mr. Stanton had called to us as we drove by. "Martha's in the house. I'll put up the horses an' be along. They need a rest anyhow."

"You ain't gotta go right away? Ye'll stay an' have supper with us?" he questioned as he came in.

12

We stayed, for the warmth and charm of the farm home made us feel as though we belonged.

"Now, I'm a man that loves my farmin', pastor, jes' like you love your preachin'. How'd ye like to slip on a pair o' overalls an' come out to the barn while I do the chores?"

In the kitchen Mrs. Stanton and I visited as we washed the dishes and separated the milk.

"Your job's a lot like a farmer's wife's, ain't it? Your husband's work wouldn't amount to much without your help," she said to me when I told her how I plan to ride the circuit with Ed.

When we finally prepared to go, they followed us to the car. "Ye'll come agin soon, won't ye?" Farmer Stanton asked. "You young folks fill an awful empty spot in this house. We had four of our own—there's jes' Marian left. She lives in the city an' don't git home often. So come out whenever ye git lonesome fer the farm."

"An' here's yer cream an' eggs," Mrs. Stanton added as she thrust a jar and a sack into my hands.

We drove home through the frosty, still night thankful for the gracious, kindly friends who fill our life.

FRIDAY, OCTOBER 22

It's late tonight. We have just returned from a full day at Gold Valley. The eerie glow of the northern lights guided our way home.

Though we were received cordially enough during the day's calling, only four elderly people came to the prayer meeting this evening—Dad Houston, the stationmaster, and his wife; Ma Thompson, whom I had met during the afternoon behind the counter of the general store; and Grandma Jarvis, alert despite her seventy years. The final

13

prayer was almost drowned out by the shouted profanities of an unruly patron being ejected from the near-by beer parlor.

"Gold Valley's a-goin' to the dogs, an' it's a-goin' fast, I tell ye," Dad Houston said vehemently. "Why, the whole town's a-livin' offen relief, an' the money's all a-spent at the beer parlors and dance halls afore any of it gits home where it belongs. But the worst is the way the young folks is a-carryin' on. Ever see any o' them in church any more?"

"I'll say not," answered Ma Thompson. "They's all down at the taverns drinkin' an' gamblin' with their dads. What can you expect o' Ken Mead's kids when they never sees their dad sober?"

"An' looka that younger Hughes girl, Evelyn," said Grandma Jarvis in a confidential tone. "Reckon she figgers if she kin get a few more customers to Barney's Place her ol' man kin up Barney's rent. As I was a-comin' to meetin' jis' now, I seen 'er sittin' at the front table in there a-drinkin' beer with young Jim Morris—an' his wife e'spectin' the third baby middle o' January."

"Whatcha gonna do, preacher?" asked Ma Thompson. "They won't listen to talk."

What are we going to do? We wonder ourselves. Poor little Gold Valley, with its meandering dirt streets, its drab, run-down little homes—many of them only tar-paper shacks with children and chickens spilling out of the front doors into the dusty streets—its two struggling grocery stores, and three thriving beer parlors, even the church badly in need of a coat of paint and a few repairs. What are we going to do?

There are the eager, wide-eyed children, like Mike and Mary Mead, and the older boys and girls, like Evelyn Hughes, who long for excitement and glamour. At least

we'll not consign them to the dogs till we first try to help them find other ways of having good times.

MONDAY, OCTOBER 25

Evenings like this deserve to be remembered. Ed had a meeting here at the Gorman church, and I spent an hour with my cello. I got out my études and velocity exercises and practiced till my fingers tingled. I forgot to pull down the front window shade, however; and about eight-thirty, while I was sawing away, I was conscious of eyes watching me. I glanced out of the window and saw half a dozen pairs of boy's eyes peering in. At my invitation the youngsters tumbled into the parsonage, bubbling over with questions about "that awful big fiddle." They listened intently while I told them of camel caravans and village drums and then played "Orientale." I told them about the swans in the city parks before I played "The Swan."

"Like them big birds we saw on Lake Lil last week," put in a curly-headed twelve-year-old, who pressed forward and came up close to gaze wonderingly at the big fiddle.

I hope the boys come back when Ed's around.

TUESDAY, OCTOBER 26

I think I'm going to like Ladies' Aids. At least I enjoyed my initiation at Gorman today. We met in the comfortable home of Mrs. Marston, the president, around the glowing fireplace of her long living room. The meeting turned into a bride's shower for me, and I came home laden with a handsome occasional chair—perhaps I can coax Ed from his comfortable old wicker rocker once in a while now— and a handful of household hints and favorite recipes. I'm sure I'll need them all.

But I think I appreciated even more the warmth of the welcome I received. Ed's remark of the other day kept singing through my mind: "It's the people who make the church; it's the people we're here to serve." And we yearn indeed to serve them well.

WEDNESDAY, OCTOBER 27

Ed came home today with a tousled, curly-headed youngster at his heels, the one who was so interested in my cello the other evening. Before Ed finished saying, "This is Warren Wilson," he headed for the few plants on the south window ledge.

"Say, do you like flowers?" he asked. "I got lots more kinds than that at home, an' mine're growin' better too. I'll bring you some."

Warren had come to see Ed's stamp collection. For an hour they buzzed about crash covers and the marvels of Zanzibar.

"I wonder how many more boys I'll find like that youngster," Ed said at lunch. "He was hanging around the pool hall when I came by, and attached himself to me because he recognized me as the new minister."

THURSDAY, OCTOBER 28

I just arranged the bountiful armful of bittersweet berries which we found in our car when we started home from Fairhaven this evening. They fill the blue vase on the preacher's filing cabinet and remind us that the season's change is in the air.

Today has belonged to Fairhaven. We left at noon in our little car and returned tonight with the great, star-filled

sky overhead and a misty new moon tangled in the clouds over the western horizon.

This afternoon we drove past the neat church to the farmhouse on the broad fields beyond.

"The Aid's meeting here at Websters' today," Ed said, as I noted the cars behind the house. Then he added, "You know, Laurie, if I were farming instead of preaching, I'd want to be the kind of a farmer Ken Webster is."

"Isn't he your official board chairman?" I asked.

"Yes. It's a trusted position for a young man to hold in a stable community like Fairhaven. You'll like his wife, Alice, too. And his father. And Grandma Webster always has just the word of encouragement her preacher needs."

The large front rooms were already filled when we got there. I found an empty chair next to Mrs. Stanton and listened to members of the Sunshine Committees give their reports.

"We sent three cards to sick neighbors at the hospital," reported the first committee.

"I called on two ailin' members an' took some chicken over to one who's bedridden."

"Mr. Miller's worse again too. We took him some magazines and cookies."

"Did you ever notice," asked the president, "how much the Bible says about the fatherless and widows? Now, we don't have many widows around Fairhaven, but we've got several widowers. Don't you suppose they'd enjoy a fresh loaf of bread or a pan of hot rolls next baking day? I've just sorta been going on the assumption that Jesus was right when He said, 'Seek ye first the kingdom of God, and his righteousness; and all these things shall be added unto you.' Or do you think we ought to talk more about raising money?"

"Guess we'll let you do it your way," answered the treasurer. "This is the first time I can remember that we've had plenty to pay the interest on the church debt and the pastor too without scraping the bottom of the till."

"An' diggin' into our pockets a little to boot," added Mrs. Stanton. "Seems a shame to be payin' more fer interest on an old debt than we're payin' our pastor."

"It ain't allus gonna be so," said old Grandma Webster from her rocking chair in the corner. "I been a-thinkin' ever' Sunday when we drive up to our little church how lucky we is to have it. We'd niver a-got it if the drouth'd set in sooner. Eight years o' dried-up crops and blowin' sands don't make life easy. But, says I, the Lord's been good to us to give us our house of worship, an' I ain't gonna complain. I'm jes' a-gonna trust in His bounty."

FRIDAY, OCTOBER 29

Ed's leaning over the table in the dining room putting bright-colored thumbtacks into our improvised map of Gold Valley. We spent the afternoon there visiting in this home and that, asking questions and collecting information. Finally we stopped at the general store and spent an hour asking Ma Thompson about her neighbors and checking on the notes we had made.

Our survey seems to be confirming our impressions. Seventy per cent of the families in the village are unchurched—have even no religious preference. In the countryside surrounding the village the percentage is much higher. Thirty-five of the forty-two families in the community are on either government relief or state old-age pension rolls. And ours is not only the only church but, except for the little two-room school, the only constructive

agency in the bewildered little town. Our hands seem weak in the face of such responsibility.

SATURDAY, OCTOBER 30

I'm proud of our little home here in Gorman. Gradually we're getting things arranged for glad and gracious living. Ed spent the morning in his temporary workshop in the woodshed making me a kitchen table.

He came in about noon with tousle-haired Warren and about four other boys. Ed didn't need to introduce the boys—Warren took over the house. Then he begged Ed to get out his stamp collection. The boys are all stamp fans. But quarrelsome! And small wonder. There's little for youngsters in Gorman that we've been able to find. The Boy Scouts disbanded a couple of years ago because of jealousies among the leaders; the 4-H club perished last year because no one cared enough to give it guidance; the public school wipes its hands of the children after the six hours of school time. But the boys have found a friend in Ed. They've found a new name for him too. To them he's "Gebby."

Yesterday Warren brought a few guppies over and gave us lengthy instructions about their proper care. He and Ed spent an hour yesterday morning fixing a habitable home for the tiny fish. In his treasure chest Ed found some coral and sea shells which a friend had sent him from the Philippine Islands. They scrubbed the pink sea shells and the pieces of blue and white coral while Ed told Warren stories of wonders beyond the seas. Warren found the Philippine stamp collection today and told his pals about water buffaloes and houses built on stilts.

The children were excited over their parsonage geog-

19

raphy lesson. Their world is one of dusty streets, pool halls, and beer parlors, high-lighted by an occasional fishing or hunting trip. They're a bickering, self-centered lot.

"How do you like our mission field, Laurie?" Ed asked after the children spilled out of the parsonage door onto the dusty sidewalk.

SUNDAY, OCTOBER 31

This was the Sabbath morning I'd been dreading at Gorman. Ed was right. Our little box of a church isn't so bad when it's full of people. Instead of the drab walls and bare floors one notices the radiant face of trim Mrs. Marston, the Gorman Aid president, the mop of white hair of Mr. Larson as he shuffles up and down the aisle ushering the worshipers to their places, the brave artistry of Mrs. Berg at the tinkly old piano, and the quiet sincerity of the Gunters as they trudge into church during the second stanza of the first hymn.

But today the benches were nearly empty. Somehow the cold barrenness of the church interior settled down like a spell over the spirits of the little handful. The church emptied quickly this morning. There wasn't the usual visiting, and we were on our way to Fairhaven earlier than usual.

TUESDAY, NOVEMBER 9

When we returned to Gorman from an afternoon of country calling today, we were greeted by a battery of snowballs and five youngsters on the run. Ed had promised to take the boys for a late fall hike, and not even a light snowfall dampened their enthusiasm. But what a time we had! They were in a quarrelsome mood. Have I ever

20

seen them when they weren't? Ed cajoled and coaxed, and after several attempts to stop the heckling he gave up. He finally decreed that each youngster must build his own fire and eat his lunch alone. I didn't eat either till I got my little fire going. The wood was damp, and the leaves were soaked, and I used seven matches. Burned fingers, singed eyebrows, and smoke-filled lungs had sobered the boys by the time we were ready to go home.

WEDNESDAY, NOVEMBER 10

Ed came in from his Gorman calling today tired and hungry. After supper we ran off to a lovely, lonely spot where overflowing lake waters have made a swamp—appropriately called Mosquito Heights—and where one is startled by the eerie cry of loons and the coarse caw of crows. We watched the teals and mallards circle above our heads and light on the quiet waters of the lake.

"You should have been with me today, Laurie," Ed said as we sat there, hanging our feet over the wall of a newly constructed dam and watching a treeful of twittering birds against the rolling clouds of the sky. "You haven't met the Koenigs yet. Calling there is like stepping into a bit of old Germany. And I know what peasant Poland is like too, after calling on Mrs. Poleski on the prairie north of town."

"All Europe out here in the sticks?"

"I didn't spend all afternoon in Europe. I stopped to see Mrs. Omann, whose husband died last fall. Five growing children and only a mother's pension to support them! Am I ever glad that those two boys have been hanging around the parsonage. Then I found the Byron home. It surely needs the friendliness of the church."

"Ed, I haven't met any of those women at the Aid meetings."

"No, I don't think our women are aware of them. Yet how they need the church!"

"Maybe that's my job. Maybe I should do a little calling."

"That's what I was thinking this afternoon, Laurie. There are two of us at this job now, you know."

Then as we drove home—the sunset full in our faces, softening the ominous clouds to a deep orchid—I had an idea.

"Ed, when the Aid meets at the parsonage next week, I'm going to ask all those women in. Take me to see them soon."

We drove homeward. The deepening sunset had wrapped our little town in its purple haze, and our hearts were full of dreams for forgotten homes.

FRIDAY, NOVEMBER 12

> We went on a hunt one winter night.
> The moon was shining awful bright,
> And we were told to come back without fail
> With a frog and a hair from a horse's tail.

So ran Dan Mead's doggerel verse written for our Gold Valley scavenger hunt tonight. I think the knot of curious parents who gathered at the church to see the youngsters return with their treasures and listen to their singing enjoyed the evening as much as the children.

How well I remember Dad Houston's vindictive remarks of three weeks ago! And how true they were! I wonder what he'd have thought of one boy's predicament when a frog got lost in his pant leg, or how he'd have settled the dispute over what constitutes a perfect ear of corn. I can

still see Dan and Leland Burton vainly trying to keep up with the actions of the song "Oh, Chester, Have You Heard About Harry?" which Evelyn Hughes was leading— Grandma Jarvis should have seen her!

Last Friday night it was a table-games tournament— African wari, Chinese checkers, and an English coin game played with real crowns and pennies.

"Say, these are swell," Leland said when we turned out the lights and shut the doors. "We'll have to teach Pop these this winter."

"Can't git over them Burton kids a-showin' up," Ma Thompson remarked to us tonight. "Why, they live three miles out in the country, an' their folks have been agin the church all their lives."

But all the town toughies were there—the hopeless town youth, consigned to the dogs three weeks ago because the town had nothing better for them.

MONDAY, NOVEMBER 15

Ed took me calling today in Gorman homes that have been acquainted with poverty and struggle and loneliness. We found Hulda Koenig and her mother threading the large rug loom by which they make their meager living. Mrs. Poleski told us in an animated mixture of Polish and English all about the ailments of her sick neighbors. At the Omanns' we found the twins and their mother eagerly planning an outing for the time when the boys would get home from their paper routes. In their modest home behind the last struggling service station on the highway the Byrons were rejoicing because they had caught enough rain in last night's drizzle for shampoos for all the family.

"The missis is in the house," Mr. Byron said to me when

I stepped out of the car. Then he motioned to Ed to sit down on the old oil can outside the door which serves as his guest chair. Life is a struggle in that little house on the village limits.

"This town don't take to strangers, Reverend," Mr. Byron said confidentially. "Take me, for instance. I had a good job in the Chicago stockyards, had a neat pile o' savin's in the bank. The depression struck. We seen we couldn't make ends meet in the city. M' wife had relatives in Minnesota. We came up here. Bought this little place. Built us a small home. Thought we could keep on top that way. But this town," he shook his head, "it's like ice. Jes' freezes folks out. You see, we ain't the right nationality. Or we don't go to the big church. But now we're caught. It's been sickness and trouble ever since we landed here. Don't know how we'll see clear through a Minnesota winter with business what it is."

In the house I found Mrs. Byron, an attractive, reticent woman, baking cookies for her children. They were as timid as little mice. As I stepped into the room, little Leila, clutching a bedraggled doll, fled into the stove corner; and tiny Davie, his wild, frightened eyes following my movements, hid behind the bedroom door.

"They're not used to strangers," Mrs. Byron apologized. "They've got no other children to play with out here, and I never get out to take them anywhere."

"Why not bring them to Sunday school?" I asked.

"It's a long way, but in nice weather I suppose I could bring them."

I issued my invitation to the Gorman Aid. She reddened and hesitated. Finally she burst forth. "Honestly, Mrs. Gebhard, it's been so long since I've been anywhere I don't think I'd know how to act. We're strangers here, and I've

24

never felt at ease since we came. It's been struggle, struggle, struggle."

"We haven't been here long either," I replied, "so I know how you feel. But I think you'll find our home a friendly place."

She finally agreed to come.

FRIDAY, NOVEMBER 19

When we awoke this morning, the ground was covered with a thin layer of frost and snow, and all day long the slate gray skies have been spitting their fury at the dismal winter world. We spent the morning at home in the study at an occupation saved for winter months—culling the parsonage files.

"Guess winter's here in earnest, Ed," I said at lunch time. "We'll get a good taste of it going to Gold Valley this afternoon."

"We won't try any country calling today. Better stop at Dad Houston's. I promised him I'd bring you around sometime. I'll find spring for you yet."

I looked at him quizzically.

"Just wait till we get there. You'll see."

So, after the dishes were done, we drove through the fitful flurries of snow and sleet to Gold Valley. We passed the bleak, unpainted church and turned at the railway station corner.

"Houstons live upstairs," Ed remarked as we crawled out of the car, "but we're stopping in the station rooms first."

We stepped into the waiting room with its long windows on three sides. It was a bower of flowers. Dad Houston came from the station office to greet us.

25

"You picked some day to come an' see my garden, preacher," he said.

"Yes, I told Laurie I'd find spring for her."

"This surely doesn't look like the rest of Gold Valley in mid-November," I said.

"I guess it don't," Dad Houston said, and his words were like the staccato of the sleet on the windows. "An' I aim that it ain't a-gonna either, missis. This town's a wicked place. There ain't much but evil an' drink left in Gold Valley. Least here Stella an' me kin keep our own doorstep clean an' our hands outa mischief."

"The town's not all bad, Dad Houston. Drop around at the church some Friday night and see the gang of youngsters who've been coming over for youth nights."

"Wal, maybe I will sometime—but one rotten apple kin spoil the whole bushel, ye know. An' from what I kin see o' this town by livin' at the end o' Main Street, the bushel's 'most rotten by now. What kin ye do with that mess o' Mead kids with their drinkin', gamblin' dad? Why, the three-year-old knows the way to Barney's Place better'n he does to home. Yes siree, Gold Valley's a-goin' to the dogs."

I looked around the room. One side was loaded with racks of cactus plants, several of them in bloom. "Growed 'em all from seed," Dad Houston said.

"Now I know where Ed has begged the shoots for his windowful of flowers," I said, spying familiar begonia and foliage plants.

"You bet. Can't keep flowers to home—not if ye love 'em like me. But here's the kinda flower you oughta grow, preacher." He pointed to a large purple bell-like blossom with petals rich and deep like velvet.

"But don't git me started on gloxinias," he warned.

"They're me favorite, an' I niver git tired of 'em. Takes three years to grow a blossom like this from a tiny speck of a seed. Course, most folks grow 'em from bulbs or slips. Not me. Niver growed a flower in me life from a bulb or slip if I could raise it from seed."

"It's really yours then, isn't it?" I said.

"You bet it is. But step into the shop afore ye go. Found some choice pieces o' diamond willow down in the Burton Bog t'other day."

He led us into the station office. It was a workshop instead. There were flower stands, table legs, and elaborate canes of gnarled willow with the diamond-shaped grooves polished out. The gray walls were lined with corner cabinets and whatnot shelves of intricate coping-saw design—here a deer leaping through the underbrush, there the symmetry of a floral pattern.

"Someone's handy with the buzz saw," I remarked as I looked around.

"Buzz saw? Say, we ain't got 'lectricity in this end o' town to read by, much less to waste sawin' with. Nope, this stuff's all done by hand." He gave it a careless glance. "An' all them patterns come outa this old head. But say, preacher, d' ye know what this is?" He gave Ed a piece of red wood.

"Why, it's cedar."

"Yep. M'son sent me this stick from the Rocky Mountains. Got a dandy piece o' black walnut over there—old organ top I picked up at a sale last week."

"And this looks like mahogany," Ed said, fingering another board that lay on the window ledge.

"Yep. I jes' been a-sittin' here tryin' to figger what I kin do with all these nice woods."

27

"You should see the table top he has upstairs, Laurie. It has over a thousand pieces of inlaid wood in it."

"Yep, but I ain't a-hankerin' fer another table top. I'll think o' sumpin, though. If you git an idee, let me know. Gotta have sumpin to keep me outa mischief." And he looked at us with sharp, intent eyes.

"Say, preacher," he said when we were ready to go, "when ye git ready to try raisin' gloxes, I'll give ye a packet o' seed."

TUESDAY, NOVEMBER 23

Well, I'm all prepared for the Gorman Aid. I've spent the morning scrubbing the fingerprints of our little visitors from the doors, washing windows, dusting around Ed's flowers on the crowded window ledge, sweeping down fuzzy cobwebs, and cleaning behind the radiators. I wouldn't want any of the ladies to inspect the closets or upset the drawers, but otherwise I'm ready for them.

I wonder how well the church women will be prepared for some of the guests I've invited. When I mentioned to Mrs. Marston the names of the women I had asked, she said, "It's nice of you to think of them, Mrs. Gebhard. But why do you use your crowded time to bother with those women? They don't keep the church going, you know."

I'm disturbed by their complacency. Perhaps if some of them could live one of my days—could go visiting in such homes as the Koenigs' and the Omanns' and see the plodding, patient way some are facing trials and troubles and sense the hopeful buoyancy of others; perhaps if they could lead a group of wide-eyed children in their play as I did this afternoon at the Junior League meeting; perhaps if they faced at their doors as frequently as I people burdened

with grief or torn with conflict—perhaps then my guests
would be more welcome.

WEDNESDAY, NOVEMBER 24

The church's folding chairs, borrowed for the Gorman
Aid meeting, are stacked again in the parsonage hallway,
and we've just lunched on leftover cakes and fruit salad.
The afternoon was a happy success.

All my guests were here. Quiet Mrs. Koenig sat in the
corner exchanging crochet patterns in rapid German with
Mrs. Berg. Mrs. Poleski arrived wearing a new dress bought
for the occasion, a prominent tag, size 44, showing above
the collar. Mrs. Omann brought a dozen eggs, "for parsonage breakfasts," she said. Mrs. Byron visited freely with
Mrs. Larson, the teacher of the kindergarten class in the
Sunday school, about her little family.

"I'll bring them next Sunday," I heard her promise.

Only one remark clouded the pleasant atmosphere of the afternoon. Our little rooms were full to overflowing with our guests. As we tried to make room for latecomers, Mrs. Larson said, "If we had a church instead of a cheesebox, we could have meetings like this there and wouldn't have to crowd into homes that are too small to hold us."

Just when I was ready to slip out to the kitchen, Mrs. Gunter said, "We'd sure like to hear that big fiddle o' yours, Mrs. Gebhard, afore ye git away." So I played to a curious, appreciative audience.

"Wonder if those women would feel more at home at our meetings if we talked less about the money we're raising?" Mrs. Larson asked while we were doing the dishes afterward.

THURSDAY, NOVEMBER 25, THANKSGIVING DAY

> Come, ye thankful people, come,
> Raise the song of harvest-home.

The families of Fairhaven gathered together in their spacious church basement, as is their custom, to keep Thanksgiving Day. Ed conducted the traditional Thanksgiving service about the well-laden board; and then in good, glad fellowship of Christian friends we enjoyed our Thanksgiving dinner, much as the early Pilgrims may have.

We took our old neighbors with us. Mr. Gunter turned to Ed on the way home and said, "Reverend, there's somethin' rightful about them Fairhaven farmers all a-comin' together to sing praises and give thanks to Almighty God fer His blessin's to His people. Yes, even in drouth years they kin say thanks to the Power that keeps 'em."

FRIDAY, NOVEMBER 26

After the Gold Valley school was out, a dozen boys tore into the church for Boy Scout meeting, forgetting even to shake the snow from their boots. The leader of one patrol, who last year quit the scouts for a while "because they were a bunch o' sissies," had an original play prepared for the boys of his group. The other patrol was ready with a demonstration of scout knots.

As I stood on the church steps watching the gang collect, little Mary Mead came rushing up to me. "Mrs. Gebhard," she burst forth, "we're gonna have a Girl Scout troop too, and you're gonna help us."

And tonight Evelyn Hughes came to me. "What do you know about Girl Scouts?" she asked.

"Only what I learned from being one."

"Oh, I just guessed you could help us. Our little girls are awfully anxious to keep up with their big brothers. They had a meeting at my house this week, and they want very much to be Girl Scouts."

I promised to help Evelyn with the group. All those children need is a leader. An older girl with Evelyn's friendly and eager personality, given a little guidance, can do much to fill their lives with more than idleness and liquor. It startles me the way the Mead children seem to dread going home. A pal's barn is a more welcome place to sleep.

SUNDAY, NOVEMBER 28

Ed rode the circuit alone this Sunday. At the Gorman Sunday-school board meeting last week I promised to visit the Gorman Sunday school. Each Sunday morning during the closing hymn I have seen the children collect outside the church for their Sunday-school session, which

31

follows the preaching service. Very often the noisy gang of junior boys climbing in the scraggly tree outside the front window or playing tag around the church has detracted somewhat from the closing prayer.

After the adults filed out of the church, the children spilled in, filling the narrow pews better than the adult congregation. A class of boys crowded into the stove corner, a group of junior-high youngsters huddled around the piano, the beginners' class gathered around their little red table in front of the pulpit, and several classes lined up in the narrow pews. I counted eight classes crowded into the small room, and the confusion of sounds rivaled the tower of Babel.

Mrs. Larson asked me to teach the kindergarten class, and I longed to teach them the little song on the back of their lesson leaflet; but instead the children and I could scarcely hear each other above the noise of the classes around us, and holding the attention of a few was like trying to teach a flock of twittering sparrows.

"Now, Laurie," Ed said at dinner, "you've been introduced to the dilemma of the one-room church."

"I've solved another riddle, Ed. I've always wondered why Mrs. Larson saves that harassed, worried look to wear to church every Sunday morning. Eight classes in that little room! Why, it's just a hubbub."

"Well, as Ma Thompson says, 'Whatcha gonna do about it?' "

I looked around the dining room. "Say, Ed, how'd it be to turn the parsonage into Sunday-school rooms? The primary class could hold forth in the living room, and the little tots in here."

"I suppose you'd like to have the little red chairs to add to our meager supply of home furnishings."

32

"Sure, and that wheezy old organ that's hiding its face in the pulpit corner."

"Well, I guess it couldn't catch any more dust here than where it is."

"Dust and old Sunday-school papers," I added.

Mrs. Larson came past the parsonage this afternoon, and I ventured our suggestion. She hesitated, fearing the imposition.

"You'll never be in our way," Ed reminded her. "We're at Fairhaven while you're at Sunday school."

So the parsonage is the new church addition.

MONDAY, NOVEMBER 29

We explored new worlds today—Gorman Grove under the fresh soft snow that fell yesterday. We cut long swaths in the unwounded surface of the snow, stood triumphant on a cliff of a snowdrift as though the world of sparkling wonder would ever belong to us, and picked our way among stairways and swings and fireplaces and tables—all deserted and silent with the hush of winter—and explored the funnel-shaped hole some curious animal had made in the white blanket as he came up to see if the shining sun meant spring was on its way.

"I'll have to try my gang of boys on these hills," Ed remarked as I sprawled headlong down a slight incline. "Those play-hungry kids!"

WEDNESDAY, DECEMBER 1

Half a dozen boys gathered at the parsonage after school today with their skis, lunch pails, and fancy boasts. They've been begging Gebby for an afternoon of skiing ever since the first frosty snow fell, and now that the hills and val-

leys of Gorman Grove are one deep unbroken stillness of white, Ed could no longer put them off.

What a bedraggled, aching crew returned for waffles and hot chocolate! I remembered their eager boasts. They were but boyish dreams that sent them tumbling and tangled down the small inclines.

"Gee, Gerry sure wanted to come," said one of the Adams brothers on the way home. "Jack and me came here, and Donnie went to the kindergarten party at Mrs. Larson's."

"Yeah," Jack added, "Ma sure had a time gettin' him t' see he was either too big or too little."

"Come on, Bill, Jack," Ed said when the others piled into the house. "We've got an errand." They returned in a few minutes, Ed leading a timid, happy seven-year-old by the hand.

"Gerry was sorta scared to come," Jack told me later in the kitchen, "but Gebby jes' walked in, picked him up, and carried him out to the car."

"And he ate more waffles than you did," said the other brother.

I listened to the stories of the afternoon's fun and made waffles till every boy was filled. How the boys adore their Gebby, and how he enjoys their young companionship!

MONDAY, DECEMBER 6

The Gorman church board met at the parsonage tonight. The snow had fallen all day, and the storm continued to rage through the evening. The meeting was a harrowing experience.

During the business session Ed asked the board about organizing a boys' club, perhaps a scout troop, among the eight or ten boys who have gathered around him to trade

34

stamps and play in his shop. I'll never forget the explosion that greeted his suggestion.

"Boy Scout troop of those boys? They're a worthless lot —not worth your effort," said one member. "Take Bill Adams, for instance. Of course you know he couldn't get any farther than the fifth grade. He's a hopeless vandal, always in trouble—and Warren Wilson isn't much better. You're just wasting your time having anything to do with those boys. Now if you had fifteen or twenty, you'd have enough for an interesting troop, and I'd be the first to say, 'More power to you.' But eight or ten—and such rascals—it can't be done."

O Jesus Christ, come back to this town and preach in Thy winsome, loving way. Tell us again the stories of the sparrows, the wild flowers, the man that causeth one of these little ones to stumble. Tell us again that the meek, the humble, the lowly minded are the blessed, are sons of our Father and brothers of Thine. Choose again fishermen, tax collectors, and humble homemakers as Thy followers, and gather Warren and Bill and the rest around Thy knees and speak Thy deathless words of wonder to their hearts.

TUESDAY, DECEMBER 7

This afternoon our old neighbor stopped at the woodshed shop where Ed was stacking our winter's supply of wood. Warren and Bill were taking turns swinging the parsonage ax. Mr. Gunter put his arms around the shoulders of the boys and spoke to Ed.

"Hope ye'll ferget the harsh words o' last night, son. I've known lots o' boys in my years, an' mark my word, the bad ones don't hang around the preacher. The kids love

35

ye, and they're learnin' to love the Master ye stand fer, an' some of us grownups are too."

WEDNESDAY, DECEMBER 8

It's eerily bright out tonight. The moonlight on the billowy snow makes day out of the night, a cold sort of northern day that doesn't invite one—or two—into the open. We're glad for the warmth of our cozy rooms, for popcorn from the Gunter garden, and for books from the study shelves.

Despite the frosty air a dozen Junior Leaguers piled into the parsonage after school today to finish the little white church model they have been making. It is standing up in front of the church altar table now, with its tall spire, stained-glass windows, and open door through which one can see the little pews and altar inside.

We were talking several weeks ago about what makes a church, and I showed the children several pictures of churches—great cathedrals and large stone edifices with open doors.

"But those are all big churches," Betty Berg remarked one afternoon. "I like little churches best because they are more friendly."

"Why can't we make a church—the kind we wish we had?" Jack Adams asked.

"I'd like to have a spire on it."

"And a bell."

"And an entranceway with nice tight doors that keep out the cold in winter."

"Can it have pretty windows—stained-glass ones, with a rose window, like the one in that picture?"

I showed the children how to make simulated stained-

glass windows by using water colors on heavy wrapping paper, then oiling the back of the paper to make it translucent.

When we had our little model completed this afternoon, we took it over to the church and put it in place. Warren dashed out and was back in a few moments with an electric light bulb and an extension cord.

"So our windows will light up and their pretty colors show," he explained.

"Can we leave it up in front of the altar table so everybody can see the kind of a church we'd like?" Betty asked wistfully.

"A little child shall lead them."

SUNDAY, DECEMBER 12

Tonight on the rustic Gold Valley altar, framed by the flickering light of two candles, was a tall calla lily, fresh from the waiting room of the railway station. On those occasional Sundays when the Houstons are not in their accustomed pew I think we miss, almost as much as their familiar faces, the offering of flowers which he always brings.

"Say, preacher," he said tonight when he came up to get his flower, "ye'd better come over an' see what I'm a-gonna do with my wood. Found somethin' to keep me outa mischief fer a while." We stopped at the station on our way home from church.

"A grandfather clock?" I questioned as we stepped into the lamplight of the station room and saw the tall framework before us.

"Sure is. There, how d'ye like that?" He handed Ed the front panel, a piece of fine-grained black walnut. Set in

37

the center in three or four contrasting colors of wood was
an exquisite twelve-pointed star.

"Why, it's beautiful, Dad Houston!" Ed exclaimed.

"Thirty-six pieces o' wood in about four square inches
there," he said, pointing to the design.

"And it looks as though it had grown that way."

"Wal, I've always wanted one o' them clocks, with long
brass weights—a-countin' off the hours. Now I'm a-gonna
have one."

I've been thinking since how each diamond and star
point is cut by hand, how the slender groove to hold each
point is hollowed out, how the pieces are matched and
fitted with a jeweler's glass, how they are glued into place
and then sandpapered till a dozen pieces look as though
they have always been united in a single lovely pattern.

Monday, December 13

Stacked behind the dining-room door are twelve little
red chairs and a little red table, for on Sunday mornings
the parsonage dining room is the kindergarten department
of the Gorman Sunday school. The old organ top holds
childish remnants of the weekly sessions: a little green mit-
ten with a bell on it, a tiny red purse, a precious book, a
rubber doll. This morning Mrs. Larson brought me two
pictures of her little class taken on the parsonage front
steps. Her most faithful pupils, she said, are little Leila and
Davie Byron, but they are so timid that Davie will not
leave her side, and Leila scarcely lifts her frightened eyes
to the other children.

She was telling the children about the White Gift Service
at the Christmas vesper next Sunday. They were greatly
excited.

"Can we sit close to the Christmas tree?" Davie asked. "In the very front row, on our little chairs," she told him. We must see that the little red chairs are there.

SUNDAY, DECEMBER 19

> *O little town of Bethlehem,*
> *How still we see thee lie!*

How still our own little village lies this blessed Christmas season beneath the quiet, star-filled sky! As we stepped from the Gorman church this evening, the peace of the Christmas music still singing in our hearts, the thin bright sliver of a new moon hung above the sunset. After it had disappeared behind the horizon, we went back to the church to pack Christmas baskets. We turned on the blue lights of the Christmas tree, and the bountiful white gifts which the congregation had brought to share with the needy looked like billowy snow about its base.

We talked of the closing climax of the service, when one by one, as I played familiar carols on my cello, the children and adults had brought their gifts to the tree.

I shall never forget little Davie Byron. Timidly he laid his gift before the tree. For a long minute he stood there, his large eyes filled with awe and wonder at the beauty before him. I fought back tears as I thought how empty Christmas would be at his house except for the gifts we would leave on the doorstep Christmas morning.

FRIDAY, DECEMBER 24, CHRISTMAS EVE

Christmas Eve! We've just returned from our Christmas calls. Out in the Fairhaven hills we took old Mr. Miller a basket of bright fruit. In Gold Valley we left the Meads a

39

box piled high with Christmas goodies, and at Grandma and Grandpa Morris' we left a little gift from the Sunday-school children and had prayer with them. On the way back we stopped at the Byrons' and left a small tree, full of lights and cookies, and a box of Christmas extras for the whole family. Then a few moments ago we paused outside the Gunters' living-room window, where a single candle made a pool of light on the snow outside, to sing a carol or two. Mr. Gunter threw open the door and asked us in. Their kind old faces shone as we told them of our Christmas errands.

"An' ye'll read the Christmas story and have prayer with us afore ye go?" Mr. Gunter asked when we were ready to leave. Ed read from the Gospel of Luke, and then in the serenity of their fellowship we prayed together.

O God, be born anew in our hearts this Christmastide. Help us remember Him for whom "there was no room." May there be none in our town who cannot see the Christmas star or hear the angels sing because their hearts are left dark through our neglect.

PART II

LATE WINTER

God lets us see his wonders;
great things he does, beyond our ken.
He bids the snow fall on the earth,
also the heavy rains. . . .
The ice forms at his breath,
and freezes the broad water hard;
he loads a heavy cloud with hail,
and from the clouds his lightning scatters.

—From Job 37 (Moffatt)

THURSDAY, JANUARY 6

Not till today had the sparrows found the Gebhard Christmas tree. But after last night's fresh snowfall the tree this morning was filled with noisy, chirping life. And on our side of the window was spring—our hyacinth blossom was filling the room with its fragrance.

As we drove home from Fairhaven late this afternoon, the white billowy clouds next to the sun reflected tall pillars of rainbow color—northern sundogs. And tonight the entire heavens were alive with the play of the northern lights. I was reminded of a sentence of Galsworthy's patrician: "It is God up there in His many moods."

FRIDAY, JANUARY 7

"Didja see them northern lights last night?" our old neighbor asked when he met Ed at the woodpile this morn-

41

ing. "Wal, ye know what that means. Better git set fer some real weather."

On our way to Gold Valley we passed the neglected service station on the outskirts of Gorman. Ed said suddenly, "Say, Laurie, don't let me forget to stop at Byrons' this afternoon. The driveway to that station hasn't been shoveled out since Christmas."

"And that's some job of shoveling," I remarked as I glanced at the snow thrown into high cliffs by the snowplow.

Later when Ed waded through the deep drifts to the Byron home, he found the family sick with heavy chest colds. Mr. Byron looked thin and worn, and his constant cough was deep and hollow.

"Have you called the doctor?" Ed asked Mrs. Byron.

"We've been trying to get on the best we can," she answered with brave pride. "With the service station out of commission we've been hard pressed this winter. It's hard for folks who've always managed by themselves to ask for help."

"The town board don't make it easy," despairing Mr. Byron put in. "They don't care much fer folks like us."

MONDAY, JANUARY 10

When the preacher came home from the Gorman board meeting tonight, his face was a perplexed study. Often after the Gorman board meetings he has a restless night. This may be another. The small group met at the church. That is a mistake, for when a few are gathered together in that dismal room, an atmosphere of chill and gloom settles down upon them in place of the blessing they should feel. Not even the little white church model up in front of the altar table made any difference.

"Don't see why we hafta send so much money off to missions an' such," spoke up the treasurer when he reported the Christmas offering. "We been doin' it fer years, an' it ain't done us here no good." He cast a disparaging look around the room.

"Another thing puzzles me," added another member of the board. "I can't understand why our preacher has to call on all the heathen at the hospital. Now we know with three churches to serve he doesn't have much time for extras. Maybe it's selfish of me, but I don't care a hang how many people you go to see at the hospital, Reverend. They don't pay anything to the church, and they haven't any right to its services."

Ed struggled through the meeting. Old Mr. Gunter sat quietly and serenely in the corner throughout the discussion. After the others had left, he spoke to Ed.

"Don't let 'em get ye down, son," he said. "I don't reckon we keep our preacher so busy preachin' us great sermons that he ain't got time to help the poor an' needy." He scratched his white head. "Don't reckon I remember of the Master askin' a man how much he could pay afore He healed 'im."

WEDNESDAY, JANUARY 12

The sun is ripening the glistening fruits of winter this bright, cold day. Every tiny twig and slender blade of grass is crystal-coated and shining. The roads are shiny too, so we were glad that today is Gorman day.

Dorothy Marston stopped in this afternoon, looking as trim as her mother. "Mrs. Gebhard," she asked, "is it hard to make windows like those the juniors made for their church model?"

I shook my head.

"I love to do things like that," she said. "Couldn't the youth group design and paint some windows like those for the big church? Couldn't the paper be glued to the panes so the light would shine through the colors?"

"I'm afraid it would be quite a task—but it might improve what we've got." I thought of the narrow arched panes of clear glass in their drab gray frames.

"And it would be fun. I think the others would like it too. Can't we talk about it at our meeting tonight?"

I spent the intervening hours searching through our art files and picture folders for pictures and articles about stained-glass windows. Ed stopped at the market to purchase a dime's worth of meat-wrapping paper.

The other young people were as enthusiastic as Dorothy, and before the evening was over, we had sketched several possible designs and symbols. One window will be dedicated to world brotherhood, with a figure of the Christ, His arms outstretched drawing all peoples to Him. We found a diagram of a stained-glass window of John Wesley preaching, the smoking factories on one side and the green fields on the other stretching into the distance. In arched letters of deep blue glass above his head were his familiar words "The World Is My Parish."

"I'd like to make a copy of that window," Dorothy remarked, and with sure strokes she began her sketch.

"Let's have a music window up next to the choir," suggested Catherine Omann, who has become an enthusiastic member of Mrs. Berg's youth choir.

"And we could put those words of Edwin Markham's on it, 'Come, let us live the poetry we sing!' "

Florence MacGregor reached for an old Christmas card from the picture file on her lap. "Here are some saucy little choir girls," she said.

I took the card and began sketching their little arched faces, lifted brows, and open mouths.

"Can't you almost hear them singing?" asked Catherine.

"Oh, you girls will have to provide the sound effects," Ed said.

MONDAY, JANUARY 17

This morning the preacher met the church treasurer on the street. "Fine sermon yesterday mornin'," he said. "Good collection too, considerin' the weather."

Then he hesitated. "Say, Reverend," he said with critical confidence, "can't you find better scripture readin's? We've heard the story of the good Samaritan ever since we were kids. We know all about that. Can't you find somethin' new and different?"

THURSDAY, JANUARY 20

Our solicitous milkman brought us sobering news along with the milk this morning.

"By the way," he said as he set down the bottle, "Mr. Byron died this mornin'. Up at the hospital. Had double pneumonia. Guess he's been a real sick man. Too bad we didn't know about the straits the family's been in."

"I've known," Ed said quietly. Then he put on his coat and hurried out to the edge of town. Mrs. Byron told him bitterly the story of her husband's death.

"Reverend," she said, "I'll never believe but what this town killed Don. He's been so discouraged since we came here. And he's had one tough break after another with the oil station."

"Yes, I know," Ed said. "Did you call the doctor after I was here the other day?"

"I waited as long as I dared. You know how it is. We've

tried to keep going without asking for help. And there wasn't any money for doctor bills. Finally Don got so bad I was scared. So I walked uptown and went to the town clerk's office to ask him how I could get a free doctor. Up to now we've always managed to pay somehow or other, and I didn't quite know how to go about asking for charity.

"Well, he and a couple of councilmen were sitting there with their feet up on the desk. When I asked them what to do, they started making smart remarks to each other about 'another charity case' and 'there goes the budget' and such. Then one of them told me that there had been too many charity cases this winter and they couldn't handle any more except emergencies until the new term starts in March."

"Did you tell them this was an emergency?" asked Ed.

"Yes, but they didn't believe me, and they were so rude about it I was ashamed to argue. So I never found out how to get a doctor on charity and just came on home."

That was Monday morning. By Tuesday afternoon Mr. Byron was so much worse that she overcame her pride and fear and went to Dr. MacGregor. He came right back with her and gave Mr. Byron a quick examination.

"We've got to get this man to the hospital," he said. "Why wasn't he taken there sooner?"

Mrs. Byron told him.

"H'm, I may have a little trouble with the town board myself," he said. "But we'll worry about that later."

At the hospital Dr. MacGregor spent hours doing everything he could for the sick man. But it was too late.

Mrs. Byron was exhausted when she finished her story. Little wonder she feels bitter and alone!

"Where's my daddy?" little Davie asked, his large bewildered eyes seeking Ed's.

Ed phoned Mrs. Marston when he got home. "Would the Aid like to send over a box of food?" he asked after he had told the story.

"Send it? I'll take it myself, and do what I can to help."

MONDAY, JANUARY 24

We climbed three flights of stairs to the funeral chapel. It's a dismal room on the top floor of the furniture store. I took my cello up, as there is no instrument up there. "Jes' never got around to gittin' an organ up here," the funeral director remarked to Ed.

A handful of neighbors and several of our church people had joined Mrs. Byron and her two children. As I played, I longed to draw little Davie, with his wild, troubled eyes, close to me and protect him from the grief that had descended upon his world. I marveled at the bravery and unbreakable pride of his mother.

Ed brought quiet comfort to Mrs. Byron. Then in measured tones he spoke to the others about the lack of neighborliness and consideration that had helped to cause Mr. Byron's death. The members of the village council, whose pompous chests had filled the doorway a few moments before, slowly backed out to a less conspicuous place in the hallway as Ed finished.

The treeless cemetery looked more barren and neglected than ever, just a forlorn corner of the prairie marked off with a barbed-wire fence. Ed and Mrs. Byron were nearly alone at the grave.

As we drove back, Ed turned to me, the weight of the sad little family on his shoulders. He shook his head. "They asked me why I read the story of the good Samaritan," he said.

WEDNESDAY, JANUARY 26

Are we ever proud of our farm! The first top bud of Ed's hyacinth began to unfold its pure white petals this morning, and by evening the delicate perfume of the buds filled the room. With reverent eyes we've watched it unfold throughout the day; tonight it's like a glowing altar candle.

And we have four tiny gloxinia sprouts in a coffee can! A month and a half ago Dad Houston gave Ed a packet of his favorite infinitesimal glox seeds. We hid the dustlike seeds in a can of fertile soil and waited for a month before the first faint speck of green showed. Now four tiny plants are unfolding their first leaves, and we dream of three years hence when we shall have earned a blossom like the velvety rose bell that greeted us at the Gold Valley service last Sunday.

Little Dale Wilson came in again this morning to measure our Easter lily sprouts on his tiptoes.

MONDAY, JANUARY 31

The preacher came in later than usual from his hospital calls today. "Found a little pal up at the hospital," he said as he came in. "Didn't know the youngster's name till today, but when I stepped into the room, he said in a weak little voice, 'I knew you'd come to see me, Jack.'"

"Jack?"

"That's been his name for me for weeks. The kid lives over in the alley behind Norb's Place, and he's often walked a block or two with me when I've gone up to the hospital. His mother was there today and looked surprised when the youngster knew me. 'He's the minister, Cary,' she said to him. Seems that the child's been talking about his friend

48

Jack for weeks. He just picks up with everyone that comes along down there where he lives. Cary insisted I was Jack. So I told him the other boys call me Gebby. 'Gebby!' he said. 'Why, Mom, that's even better than Jack, isn't it?' "

"Who is the youngster, Ed?"

"The Mills boy. Has pneumonia. He's been a sick little fellow, and from the looks of the shack he lives in, I'm not surprised. By the way, I invited his mother to the next Aid meeting. Told her you'd be glad to call for her. She said she'd like to come—would come often, except that her husband's had a slack season with his trucking business, and she sometimes just doesn't have the money for the lunch."

"We hear that frequently, don't we?"

"That's another Gorman dilemma, Laurie."

FRIDAY, FEBRUARY 4

Home again from bickering, bewildered little Gold Valley, with the weight of its troubles on our shoulders. Our youth nights must be cutting deep. Barney's Beer Parlor has decided to hold weekly dances—following the church youth nights! And the village council has granted the liquor stores permission to extend their closing hours from eleven till one on Friday nights. "If that blankety preacher would get out of town," said one of the tavern proprietors, "maybe we could do some business."

Only a few girls were out to scout meeting this afternoon —and their minds were on the dance tonight. Evelyn Hughes was much disheartened. As she concluded her excellent demonstration in first aid, she grumbled something about whether it had been worth while to decline an invitation the night before to prepare it for so few. Perhaps a leader needs followers as much as followers need a leader.

My heart aches for the children and young people who

49

grow up beneath the shadow of the saloon, knowing no fun but that of the dance hall and tavern, and knowing no homes but those soaked through with liquor. I look at lovable little Mary Mead, and Mike, and Dan, and toddling Patsy Mead. What can the future hold for them—with their father drinking up the dimes that should buy them milk and clothing? And there are a dozen other homes like theirs in Gold Valley. Only God in His infinite wisdom and understanding can guide us. *O Lord, how long? How close to Thee we must live—we who attempt to interpret Thy spirit in beaten, battered little communities like Gold Valley.*

Tonight as we drove home, sharing our perplexity, the full moon shone on the snow-laden tamaracks in the swamp. Ed turned to me with the words of the poet:

> "The full moon is the Shield of Faith:
>   As long as it shall rise,
> I know that Mystery comes again,
>   That Wonder never dies,
>
> .   .   .   .
>
> That utmost darkness bears a flower,
>   Though long the budding-time." [1]

WEDNESDAY, FEBRUARY 9

Today the outside world was a mist of unending white— the sky above, the snow, the shrubbery, the fence posts, and the trees. Each tuft of grass bore its filigree of lace, each tree its burden of feathery finery. There were not even shadows to break the white monotony.

But within the warmth of our walls was color: all the rich blues and purples, warm reds and browns which we

[1] Vachel Lindsay, "The Shield of Faith," from *Collected Poems*, published by The Macmillan Co.

could coax from the paint box for our stained-glass window designs. Dorothy and her group have spent many hours drawing John Wesley, and tonight they began lettering the deathless words above his head. Catherine, Florence, and I have been eager to get our little choir girls, with their stiff surplices, properly painted and enameled. Now the first copy is done and hangs on the dining-room wall in all its saucy glory.

MONDAY, FEBRUARY 14

We visited little Cary Mills today. He was sitting up in the big chair with his father's overcoat wrapped about his thin little body. He's still a sick, but very cheerful little boy. He had a large wallpaper sample book on the table in front of him and was making valentines. We came home laden with wallpaper tokens of boyish affection.

His is a humble, brave little home. It sits just off the alleyway behind Norb's Place, little more than a shack, built of old lumber that's had no acquaintance with paint. But inside the modest furnishings are attractively arranged and bravely clean. On one wall hangs a landscape by one of the Flemish masters, clipped from a magazine and mounted behind glass with black electrician's tape.

Mrs. Mills is a pleasant, hard-working young woman, very devoted to her little son and their home. Mr. Mills evaded us. He is a rough-and-ready sort of fellow. His embarrassment at our visit was a startling contrast to Cary's eager welcome.

"Cary's better, don't you think?" Mrs. Mills asked Ed. "It's been a hard winter for us. Business has been poor, and Cary's been sick most of the time. But we have the truck paid for now. If we only have a good blueberry season next summer!"

42913
MANCHESTER COLLEGE

"Blueberry season?" I asked. "Do you go blueberrying?"

"In a rather big way. You see, for years Ernie and his father have gone up to the border, where they buy blueberries from the Indians and truck them to the city. My job comes in managing the exchange we set up in camp."

"Gee, it's fun!" Cary exclaimed.

"Cary loves it. We drive the truck deep into the woods on an old railroad bed and set up camp near where the Indians pick berries. It's lonely, but interesting. If we just have a good season next summer, we can really begin living."

MONDAY, FEBRUARY 21

When I cleared the table of supper dishes, there, framed between the two candles, were Ed's narcissus with their perfect blooms.

"Leave them there," Ed said. "They might change the atmosphere of the Gorman board meeting tonight."

But that was expecting too much. Gold Valley was up for discussion before the regular business session began, and

we were telling the group about the competition we were encountering with our youth nights.

"That's a waste of time," remarked one of our community leaders. "Why meddle with them? The whole town's no good. I learned my lesson. Went down there to help out one night in a community program. How did they thank me? They let the air out of my tires. I haven't been down there since. You can't change a town like that."

"It's the biggest collection of no-accounts I ever seen," added another. "No good'll ever come from that town."

"Well, maybe you're right," Ed finally said, "but it's my job to try." Then he read for his meditation that passage of scripture where Jesus tells the Pharisees that he came not for those who had no need of a physician, but for the sick.

TUESDAY, FEBRUARY 22

> *"The day will bring some lovely thing."*
>
> . . . .
>
> *Each night I pause, remembering*
> *Some gay, adventurous, lovely thing.*[2]

Pools of yellow light on the snow beneath the street lamps. Winter dusk with wet wind in my face.

The traceries of twigs against the darkening sky.

The moon, lighting up the clouds that cover its face.

The delicate odor of our first freesia blossom, dew-wet and half open on its slender stem.

Ed's delightful watch over the flowers on the crowded window ledge. He places and exchanges the pots of growing plants, seemingly just to show that tender concern which cannot leave its loves alone.

[2] From *Songs for Courage* by Grace Noll Crowell, copyright 1938 by Harper & Brothers.

WEDNESDAY, FEBRUARY 23

This morning, while I was in the midst of my breakfast dishes, a woman and two men from Gold Valley came to the door. They seemed quite perturbed as they asked for Ed. Soon we heard the whole story, and we understood their agitation.

They were the Mead family—the grandfather, uncle, and mother of the neglected little brood who have flocked to the scout troops and youth nights. Last night Ken Mead, their father, had a tragic accident with his truck. It cost him his life.

"Drunk?" Ed questioned.

"Yes," Ken's father replied heavily. "He and his pal had made the rounds of the taverns in Milltown, Gorman, and Gold Valley, and on the way home—"

"You might as well know," his brother put in. "His friend Al was so liquored up he didn't know what had happened when they found him in the wrecked truck."

"Will you take the service, preacher?" the woman asked. "We know it will be difficult, but we'd like it at the church." She was broken with grief and shame.

Ed was silent for a few moments. When he answered, he spoke gravely. "Yes, I will take the service—under one condition." He hesitated. "I want you to understand that in part of the message I will try to bring comfort to you and your little family. But in part of the message I want the privilege of attacking this evil that's cost your husband's life—and I'll attack it hard."

FRIDAY, FEBRUARY 25

Gold Valley went to the Mead funeral today. The whole town was there. Those who could not crowd into the little

church gathered around the windows to watch from the outside. I scanned the faces of the crowd from my seat with the quartet on the platform.

This is Gold Valley, I thought. Tired, tense little Gold Valley. Ed was right. "Laurie," he has often said, "they're like wild deer breaking into town."

The back rows and aisles were crowded with farmers and townspeople dressed in their clean clothes. In the front row sat Ken's dad, looking older and tireder than I had ever seen him look, and Mrs. Mead with her pitiable little family filling the row. Dan, next to his mother, sat through the whole service staring blankly past the casket. Twelve-year-old Mary hid her own perplexity in the solicitous care she gave little Patsy. Mike's tear-stained face did not leave Ed's all of the time he spoke.

To the left sat the pallbearers, all of Ken's drinking pals. How frequently we have seen them hanging around outside Barney's or Pat's beer parlor while their families in the tar-paper shacks went without milk and shoes!

As the quartet sang "Beautiful Isle of Somewhere," Ma Thompson's old question plagued me like a worn phonograph record stuck on the question, "But, Reverend, whatcha gonna do? They won't listen to talk. Whatcha gonna do?"

Ed fulfilled his promise. His message to the pitiable little family was compassionate and kind. Then, with one eye on the row of pallbearers, Ed lashed out forcefully against the evil that is sapping the lifeblood of Gold Valley. "The wages of sin is death," he quoted. He proceeded to point out that we must live by the laws of God or perish.

The congregation was hushed and still. I watched the men on the front row. As Ed reached the climax of his message, they were getting uncomfortable and angry. At the ceme-

tery Ed parked his car carefully so he could get away immediately.

As Ed was crawling back into the car, Ken's father came up to him and offered him a handful of bills.

"I can't take anything for this service," Ed told him quietly. Then, as Mr. Mead hesitated, he added, "Give your money to his brave little wife."

SUNDAY, FEBRUARY 27

The portrait of "The Son of Man" on our living-room wall blesses the whole room with its spirit. We came in from the Gold Valley service tonight, and I threw myself into the rocking chair opposite the picture. There in the half-darkened room, although I could not make out the features, I could feel His presence, and I worshiped beneath the compassionate gaze of the Master.

How out of harmony our world—or even, at times, my own little world—seems beneath the gaze of the Christ! How great looms the task to which Ed and I have dedicated our lives!

At the service tonight we were a bit perplexed to see in the congregation the faces of several men who do not often attend church. We knew the memory of Friday's funeral was fresh in the minds of all. After the service the preacher shook hands with a genial congregation, but the men held back. When the church was nearly empty, they approached Ed. Young Jim Morris led the procession. He took Ed's hand in a vigorous grasp.

"We all heard that service Friday," he said, "and we know you didn't have an easy job. We just want you to know that you're the kind of a preacher we want in this town."

He left a dollar bill in Ed's hand. Each of the men as he went out did likewise. Our gratitude is deep for their thoughtfulness.

WEDNESDAY, MARCH 2

Every bush and tuft of grass tonight bears a fairy burden of white loveliness after today's snowfall. Our own little problems seem like fairy burdens too, for today, with the morning mail, came the first hint of spring. The first seed catalogue, with its dreams of summer fruitfulness, arrived. Ed and our old neighbor have spent the afternoon planning their gardens.

"Gardens make dreamers of us all, son," Mr. Gunter said as he rose to go. "Mebbe that's why the good Lord planned for seedtime an' harvest."

WEDNESDAY, MARCH 9

I went down to the alley behind Norb's Place to pick up Mrs. Mills for the Gorman Aid meeting. She enjoyed the friendliness of the women. "You don't feel as though you're standing alone—in a group like that," she said to me when I left her.

Only one bit of discussion clouded the pleasantness of the afternoon. Mrs. Marston, the president, ventured the suggestion that, with the youth choir in their new white surplices and the new designs which the youth group have put on the windows, it would be a good idea to clean the church before the Lenten Vesper Service a week from Sunday.

"That's about the most discouraging place to clean I ever saw," answered Mrs. Berg. "Cleaning won't lay new floors, or make the window frames fit better, or paper the dirty old walls."

"Or give us enough room for Sunday school or church suppers," put in Mrs. Larson.

"Well, it will get the dust off the moldings and the cobwebs out of the corner above the pulpit and the year's collection of grit off the windows," answered Mrs. Marston. "And my vacuum cleaner is straining to get at the dusty carpet on the platform."

"And the old cabinet with torn paper costumes stacked on top and old Sunday-school papers spilling out on the floor below surely is a challenge to my wastepaper basket," said Mrs. MacGregor, the doctor's wife.

"Wish we had a church worth cleaning and caring for. But that old box!" murmured Mrs. Larson to Mrs. Berg.

Despite the mumblings the ladies were invited to bring their mops and scrub pails, furniture polish and dust cloths, to the church next Monday.

SUNDAY, MARCH 13

Tonight at the Gold Valley service, when the preacher prayed, "God, we would come before Thee with clean hands and a pure heart," Mike Mead held up two mud-soaked hands to Ma Thompson.

"They was clean when I left home," he whispered. "Honest, they was! But my ball rolled into a mud puddle on the way to church."

It seems good to have the ice melt enough to make a few mud puddles.

MONDAY, MARCH 14

Strange things come to light on church cleaning days. While the other Gorman women swept down cobwebs, replaced burned-out light bulbs, and mopped the dusty floors, I cleaned the old cabinet behind the stove. Beneath the

disarray of old Sunday-school papers and worn-out hymnals I found a tin birthday cake, some candles hungry church mice had nibbled, a bundle of revival songbooks, last year's youth-conference poster, and some church records.

I brought the records home, thinking Ed could discard those of only transitory value. Among other things we found the complete list of ministers who have served this charge and their years of service. The list was long, for a church just past its golden anniversary. In fact, to our amazement we found that in fifty-three years the longest pastorate had been two and a quarter years.

"I guess I know why," Ed remarked. "The church board's frozen them out."

"Or starved them into leaving."

"Think we can take it, Laurie?"

"Well, we have a warm house."

"And if Mr. Gunter has his way, we'll have a big garden."

SUNDAY, MARCH 20

As the afternoon shadows lengthened and the softened rays of sunlight streamed through the church windows, the Gorman congregation gathered for the Lenten Vesper. Twenty-five choir girls wearing white surplices and carrying lighted candles marched down the simple church aisle. Their music was beautiful. I had almost forgotten the joy of complete abandon which came as I drew from my cello deep warm tones of the music I so love. From the opening strains of the processional to the closing bars of "Now the Day Is Over" and Ed's benediction, the hour was one of supreme beauty.

And our windows helped. Everyone felt the warmth of the softened, diffused light. The designs and symbols

spoke their message too from the bars of "Blest Be the Tie That Binds" on the music window to the figure of the winsome Christ with the yearning nations at His feet. Of course our workmanship is amateurish and full of mistakes, but it's an attempt to beautify something that was drab and unlovely, and that is co-operating with God.

I remember Dorothy's wistful question after we got the windows all in place yesterday, "Do you think it'll help folk see what might be?"

Jesus told a story once about leaven.

PART III

SPRING

For, lo, the winter is past,
the rain is over and gone;
The flowers appear on the earth;
the time of the singing of birds is come,
and the voice of the turtle is heard in our land.

—Song of Songs 2:11-12

FRIDAY, MARCH 25

The quarter moon is shedding its magic light over the snow—worn-out snow that looks fresh and wonderful only beneath the charm of the moon.

My Gold Valley girls and I found spring today. And what discoveries! Hepatica buds hidden under brown leaves, the first pussy willows in their furry softness, green clover at the edge of snow that melted only yesterday, a jaunty woodpecker at his springtime work, a gray squirrel chasing his shadow, slaty juncos flashing their white taillights, birds' nests begging for occupants, winter buds swelling and unfolding. We felt like true explorers.

Evelyn had gone ahead to lay the trail which led to the discovery of these wonders.

"Never dreamed what fun scouting would be," she said to me this afternoon. "Am I ever glad I can help these kids have some fun I missed when I was their age."

Dad Houston stopped us after the Gold Valley choir practice tonight. "I was a-lookin' fer you folks all afternoon. Got sumpin' to show you afore ye go home t'night."

61

We drove over to the old railway station.

"Shucks," Dad Houston exclaimed as we stepped into the dark hallway, "I shoulda sent fer ye this afternoon. But Stella'll bring a lamp in a minute."

Soon Mrs. Houston came down the stairs with a flickering coal-oil lamp, and we followed its dim yellow light into the dark workshop and over to the west window. There, filling the window ledge, were gloxinias—a dozen plants laden with rich, full blossoms.

"Forty-five blossoms on 'em this afternoon, and more fat buds a-ready to pop," boasted Dad Houston. "Lookee here!" His hand trembled as he held the lamp close to a deep purple bloom with a pure white center. "How's that fer a flower? Or here?" He bobbed the lamp over to a cluster of eight deep red bells on a single plant.

As our eyes became more accustomed to the dim light, we saw new wonders of form and color on the window ledge, a rainbow of velvety loveliness.

When we got home this evening, Ed stepped over to the south window and examined the tiny plants in the coffee can. "I guess they've still got a little to go," he mused.

MONDAY, MARCH 28

If a stranger had looked into the parsonage living room this morning, he might have thought the preacher had started a kindergarten. Another youngster followed him home and came in to see the bowlful of tiny guppies.

Mrs. Mills stopped Ed on the street yesterday. "Cary's smaller than the other boys in your group," she said, "but he's been begging to go along when you take the boys for outings. Couldn't you include him?"

Ed laughed. "First thing I know I'll have to organize a kid brother's club."

She smiled. "Cary'd like to be a charter member of that," she said. "I don't know whether you realize it or not, Reverend, but what you're doing for these children in the church is the only thing of that kind in town. And you know how Cary needs it. You've been down our alley."

So Cary came over too, with his new sailor hat. And Dale Wilson dropped in just to make sure there was no favoritism, and Donnie Adams stopped by with his hands full of fish for the preacher's dinner. Ed made coins disappear and played "Hide the Nickel" with his kindergarten class till I called lunch.

SUNDAY, APRIL 3

A day of worship at our country altars is over. I can still hear the Gold Valley congregation sing "Day Is Dying in the West" as the setting sun flooded the west windows of the church.

The Burtons have been coming to church occasionally. I remember Ma Thompson's surprise last fall when Leland and Irene began attending the youth nights. "Why, when they lived in town, their pa wouldn't even let 'em come to Sunday school. 'A lotta tommyrot,' he used to say."

But tonight Mrs. Burton moved up to the organ stool. There she belongs. When she starts to sing, I'd like to silence everyone else and listen to her alone. Her voice is rich and vibrant, clear and pure like a full-toned bell. And she sings because she loves to sing. She's had no training, but she plays the organ as she sings—her whole spirit relaxed and responsive to the message of the music.

Mr. Burton's reaction to the service was an interesting contrast. The first evening he attended church, it was plainly against his will, as though he came to protect his family from any nonsense. At first he seemed cynically

63

amused by the service; he sat in the rear of the church, leaning back on a straight chair, a very critical spectator. Tonight he moved up to the front row beside Leland and Irene. I thought at first that my preacher's winning way had won—until the service began. He was attentive as I played a prelude of evening hymns on my cello. During the first hymn Mrs. Houston offered to share her songbook with him. He was rude in his refusal. During the pastoral prayer he coughed and cleared his throat till Ed could scarcely be heard. And when Ed began to preach, he shuffled his feet. Finally he reached for a Sunday-school paper, which he noisily crumpled.

"Why do you suppose he comes to church?" I asked on the way home.

Ed smiled. "Because he can't stay away, Laurie."

I wonder how long he can resist the power of the winsome Christ.

THURSDAY, APRIL 7

A white world greeted us this morning. It soon became gray, however, and stayed a quiet, rainy gray all day. We plowed through the mud to the Fairhaven crossroads, where the church people had gathered to set out trees and shrubs around the neat white church.

"The drouth was pretty hard on the church trees," remarked Grandpa Webster, "but we kin keep a-tryin'. Someday we'll git our little church in the shade."

The Fairhaven folk love their country church. They love the shiny varnished floors and the substantial oak pews, the trim dignity of the pulpit, with the circular stained-glass window above it. They love the airy, large basement and well-equipped kitchen. They love their church, and they take loving care of it.

After school little Louise Webster came trudging over to the church with lunch pail, school satchel, and a boxful of baby rabbits. Her daddy had rescued them from the plow yesterday while he was working in the fields. She

gave us a special demonstration of how to feed baby rabbits with a medicine dropper.

"We're going to have a rabbit hunt out at our place," she announced. "You see, all my friends in the first grade begged for one of my rabbits. So I just decided to let them come out and find their own."

FRIDAY, APRIL 8

When I stepped into the car after the Gold Valley Girl Scout meeting, I found my half of the seat usurped by to-

65

mato plants and brilliant foilage shoots. I knew where the preacher had been.

"We're going to Houstons' for supper," Ed remarked when he came out of the church. "The clock's finished, except for the works, but you'll have some game of hide-and-seek ahead of you before you find it."

"Dad Houston's hidden it?"

"Yes. Till it can chime the hours for his visitors."

I found it at last, hidden behind the door of the back storage room. I stood before the rich black walnut case with its finely fashioned designs in birch and maple, thinking of the story that each piece might tell. An old organ top, a hickory log from the Ozark hills, a mahogany bedstead, white birch from Minnesota's north woods, a piece of maple from an old cradle—each has a history of its own blended together by Dad Houston's skill.

Dad Houston has been so busy on his clock that he's hardly taken time from his work to eat. But he still lends his rich bass to the Gold Valley choir. Everyone enjoyed tonight's choir practice. The Burtons were there. Mrs. Burton played the organ and led out in her strong, clear voice. I had my cello along—we called on old Grandpa Morris this afternoon, and he had asked me to play for him—and I played along with the choir tonight.

Mr. Burton sat in the last row again, all by himself. He listens intently, as if he is taking it all in. Mrs. Burton has an appreciative audience in him—and so have I.

After our rehearsal he came up to me. "You folks could bring that big fiddle and find your way out to our place. 'Twouldn't hurt you and Vera any to get together."

"Say," remarked Ed on the way home, "that's an invitation we're going to accept."

MONDAY, APRIL 11

After school Warren came over to celebrate his birthday. He brought his fish spear along, and he had borrowed Bill's for the preacher. "The suckers're runnin' swell," he said.

There was a cold northwest wind, but the blue skies and twittering birds acclaimed it spring anyway. The watery bogs were already abloom with little clumps of marsh marigolds. While Ed and Warren stopped at the dam to watch the bullheads bump their blunt faces against the grating, I went bird hunting.

A catbird played its sassy tricks on me; a green heron skittered down to the lake near by; red-winged blackbirds pestered a great crow at her nest; several goldfinches flitted among the budding bushes—some had doffed their olive-green garb, others were still somberly arrayed.

When we got home, Ed gave Warren the scout book we had bought for him. He was an excited boy. He leafed through it in the midst of our waffle supper.

"Look!" he exclaimed. "A merit badge for raisin' pigeons. I thought the only thing pigeons were good for was to shoot at."

Ed laughed. "You may find some more surprises in that book."

FRIDAY, APRIL 15

I just looked at the moonlight on the front-room floor and came to bed laden with the alarm clock and a dish of grapes. Ed came in from Gold Valley a few minutes ago.

"Laurie," he said, "this was a red-letter day for little Gold Valley. Evelyn Hughes is going to do a good job as recreation director for the town. She has a good committee to stand by her; the mayor, the schoolteacher, Ma

Thompson, Grandma Jarvis, and Evelyn's father, who offered the use of his vacant store building for a community center.

"Preacher," Mr. Hughes had said, "I ain't a churchgoin' man, but you showed us. I wouldn't a' believed the kids o' this town would run to a church program sooner 'n a dance if I hadn't a-seen it with m' own eyes."

"You bet!" the old mayor exclaimed. "It ain't dancin' an' drinkin' that takes with these kids no more. An' I don't mind a-sayin' I'm mighty glad fer the change."

Tonight they planned ping-pong tournaments, kittenball teams, handcraft activities, and extended scout programs. They dreamed of tennis courts for the summer, a skating rink for winter. And each left the meeting determined to use his influence among his friends and neighbors to make their dreams come true.

"Why, if this'd happened half a dozen years ago," said Mr. Hughes, "you'd a' niver preached that Ken Mead funeral sermon."

THURSDAY, APRIL 21

Country calling was on the schedule today. The balmy spring sunshine sent us exploring the maze of roads and trails near Fairhaven that wind around lakes and over sand hills to homes that have been snowed in all winter. Ed would often go out to the shop or barn or wait at a corner of the field where the men were plowing, and I would knock on the kitchen door and visit with the women. Then we would compare notes afterward.

"This is a German community," one woman said to me. "We're Swedes, and we don't quite fit."

An hour later and two miles down the road another

woman remarked, "Here we are Germans in a Yankee community. No wonder we're sorta outa things."

Chore time found us near the Websters', so we stopped there for supper. Ed donned overalls and helped Ken and his father with the milking, while I played with Louise and Doug on the front-room rug—and chatted on the side with Grandma in her rocking chair—till Alice was ready to have me set the table.

After supper Louise said eagerly, "Do you want to come out and see my lambies?" We followed her to the enclosure beyond the barn. "Come 'ere, Blacky," she called as she leaped over the fence and grabbed the awkward, long-legged lamb. She made another dash and brought Whitey up to the fence.

"They're such wriggly little bundles!" she cried as they squirmed out of her tight grasp. "Daddy gave them to me for my very own."

We had to see her garden too. A little square next to her mother's flowers holds what she herself chooses to grow.

"I planted peanuts last year," she told us.

"I wish all parents were as wise as Ken and Alice," Ed said as we drove away.

FRIDAY, APRIL 22

> *April, April,*
> *Laugh thy girlish laughter;*
> *Then, the moment after,*
> *Weep thy girlish tears.*[1]

Such have been these lilting spring days. But the windy rain in the morning air cleared by the time we left for

[1] William Watson, "April," from *The Poems of Sir William Watson, 1878-1935*, published by George G. Harrap & Co., Ltd.

Gold Valley and let us spend the whole afternoon calling in the homes without getting caught in a shower.

We stopped by to see Grandpa Morris, whose old hands were busy whittling doll furniture for his great-granddaughter.

Afterward we went up on the hill, where old Grandpa Simmons is suffering from a stroke. Ed read from the Bible and prayed with the old couple. Grandma Simmons, who lives in the dark world of the blind, seemed greatly strengthened by the scripture and prayer.

In our visit with Mrs. Hughes I sensed for the first time a real friendliness in her attitude. Heretofore she has shown a courteous interest in Evelyn's activities, but something has seemed to keep us at a distance with her. We had expected to find the older daughter, Doris, who has been home for two weeks from her work in the city, but Evelyn had taken her to help prepare for the scout meeting. Mrs. Hughes was alone with tiny gray-eyed Donnie, who sat in the doorway singing a lusty lullaby to a white kitten. As we left, I paused for a few moments to play with him.

Then tonight I wish that Dad Houston might have looked in on the knot of twenty boys and girls gathered about our campfire in the woods. Perhaps he would change his mind about the sad plight of Gold Valley youth.

There was the spirited treasure hunt as darkness fell, with the flaming fire in the clearing awaiting the successful searchers. There were the circle games and action songs in which all participated like awkward young colts. There were the marshmallows, most of them burned to a crisp yet consumed with great gusto. Then as the fire sank to a bed of glowing embers and the star-studded sky seemed to settle down like a canopy above our heads, the group began

singing spontaneously some of the Negro spirituals we have been learning, and they waited expectantly for the story which followed.

All the town rowdies were in the circle—and lost themselves completely in the joyous activities of the evening.

We put the fire out and started back to town as the great orange moon arose over the horizon. Doris Hughes hung back, and I waited for her. She's an attractive girl, prettier than Evelyn but seemingly less vivacious. She has seemed especially to enjoy being with the others on the youth nights, although at times she has been strangely reticent and thoughtful.

We sauntered back to town more conscious of the stars overhead than of the village lights beyond.

"It was fun tonight, wasn't it?" I said, breaking a long silence.

"It was wonderful." She paused. "Mrs. Gebhard, I've been thinking all evening how lucky Evelyn is. If there'd just been something like this a few years ago, maybe I wouldn't have made such a mess of things."

We walked along in silence again.

"You're going back soon, Doris?"

"Yes. And I hate it." Her tone was bitter. "It's work, work, work—in somebody else's house with somebody else's kids around my skirts. It's like leaving a part of myself behind—leaving Mother and Donnie. If only I could have him with me!"

"Why?" I asked, remembering the tiny gray-eyed boy and his white kitten.

"Mrs. Gebhard, I guess Mother hasn't told you. Donnie's my boy."

WEDNESDAY, APRIL 27

Whoever plants a seed beneath the sod . . .
He trusts in God.

We made garden today. Last week we found the first pale lavender crocuses in their furry petaled coats, and today we hid some little brown seeds in the ground, potent with new life. The brown earth, warmed by the same sun that's been coaxing our spirits to fresh growth, will do wondrous things to the little seeds we entrusted to it. Soon there will be red radishes, green lettuce with curly edges, the first sweet garden peas. Soon we'll watch God grow in our garden—watch Him rise and smile in the bronze of marigolds and wave His arms in tiger lilies and sweet peas and unknown surprises. Gardens hold good things, and folk who work in gardens learn the joy of working with God.

SUNDAY, MAY 1

The spring drizzle kept Gorman worshipers at home this morning. Just a handful gathered in the bleak, damp church for the preaching service. And again Ed's sermon, which was later received with such eager expectancy at Fairhaven, at Gorman seemed to fall on deaf ears.

"I hope the spring sun can thaw out that Gorman congregation," Ed remarked as we drove through the muddy roads to the Fairhaven church.

"Have you noticed that Mrs. Mills and Cary have been coming to church lately?" I asked.

"Yes, and Pop Larson, my head usher, has noticed it too."

"Oh?"

72

"He shook his white head at me on the way out this morning. 'Say, Reverend,' he said, 'how come that Mills kid an' his ma are a-comin' to church?'

" 'Why?' I asked.

" 'Well, they ain't exactly church people. Seems sorta queer to see folks like them a-comin' to church. Guess a little churchgoin' won't hurt 'em though.' "

MONDAY, MAY 2

Today is Monday, and it's been a real "preacher's Sunday." When the Gorman church board meeting was postponed, Ed said, "Let's celebrate. Let's run off to the park." Off we went, as excited over our unexpected holiday as two children dismissed from school.

It has been a day filled with keen delights: steak and fried potatoes over the campfire, tall forest giants with their eternal gray-green foliage and the fresh new green in the grasses at their feet, a branch of wild plum in flower against the placid blue-green lakes of the park. We pushed through the native underbrush to the headwaters of the Mississippi and climbed the hundreds of stairs to the vista atop the forestry tower. Then coming home there was the sunset with spruce tips against it, and moonlight, and each other.

We needed to get away from our dusty Gorman concerns. We needed to rediscover our inner poise and peace beneath the night skies. Life with Edward is a high privilege. And somehow God, in the wonder of His fellowship, is indeed a frequent guest in our little home.

And as usual, when we have paused for a reflective look at our work, our imaginations have been playing with new ideas for our little churches.

73

"Laurie," Ed said on the way home, "what would you say if I stopped in at Midland next week and talked to the architect about our Gorman church dilemma?"

"Why don't you? Sometime the Gorman church will burst its drab cocoon."

WEDNESDAY, MAY 4

Tonight we took Warren and Bill over to Gold Valley with us to see Dad Houston's workshop. The grandfather clock is finished. The heavy brass weights, the delicate lettered face, and the singing chimes that peal off the quarter hours do justice to Dad Houston's workmanship. We stayed longer than we intended in order to listen to the music of the chimes.

Dad Houston handed Ed a panel of mahogany with a floral design begun in lighter woods.

"What's this?" Ed asked.

"Jes' got my appetite whetted with that clock," Dad Houston replied. "That's got five hundred pieces in the inlays. This un'll have a thousand. It'll be ten inches taller, and I'm orderin' out some deeper chimes—real basso ones. The pattern's gonna be all flowers—got some birch an' ash an' maple fer 'em." He pointed to the heart-shaped petals and the intertwining stems of the design.

"Whatcha gonna do with all the clocks?" one of the boys asked.

"Wal, I dunno," he drawled. "Think I'll jes' keep 'em a-settin' around here till I git me fill o' hearin' them chimes mark off the hours."

FRIDAY, MAY 6

The woods are togged out in their fresh green finery now, and all the way to Oak Point the Gold Valley Girl Scouts identified birds, chased butterflies, and gathered wild flowers. The waxy petals of bloodroots, the humming insects, ducks going north, jaunty blackbirds riding their water reeds, blue violets shy and hidden in the swamp grass, an old turtle's curious survey of its world—all spell spring in nature's alphabet. Despite the chilly wind from the lake we relished our outdoor supper.

We got back to the church just as the first cars arrived for choir practice. Several young people were there. All the lovely melodies that the Gold Valley choir is practicing for their Mother's Day Musical keep mixing themselves into a medley of music and singing themselves over and over in my mind.

Gathered around the old organ in the little church were white-haired Grandma Jarvis, brow wrinkled, mouth agape, intent on the alto notes; unkempt Dan Mead singing a rich monotone; earnest Evelyn Hughes; and the group of happy children, enthusiastic about their special part in the program. On the organ stool was Mrs. Burton, leading out in her clear, pure soprano. The Burtons brought a recruit for the choir tonight, a neighbor "from the next farm south," who also loves to sing. The farmer, clean-shaved and dressed in his best overalls, added a singing tenor to Dad Houston's resounding bass.

"I may be kinda rusty," said the neighbor when Mrs. Burton introduced us. "I ain't done much singin' lately— except to the cows."

The program Sunday will be simple, but it will have that reverent beauty that a task earnestly and humbly done often possesses.

WEDNESDAY, MAY 11

The preacher came in this afternoon with a precious package tucked under his arm. The architect's suggestions have at last arrived! Edward spent the afternoon poring over them. And then tonight after supper when we went

out to our garden plot, the plans were riding around in his back pocket.

The first peas are stretching their tendrils into the sunlight, and there is a fringe of green down the lettuce row. Ed pushed aside the small humps of earth on the row marked "beans" to show me that the first leaves were unfolding.

Old Mr. Gunter was scratching about the gladiola spears when Ed called him. We picked our way between rows of radishes and onion sets. Ed rolled out the precious plans against the Gunter barn. As Mr. Gunter studied them, I glanced across the fields to the forsaken little church building. In a few moments he looked around at Ed, a smile flooding his face.

"Son," he said, "you're a-plantin' sumpin besides beans an' carrots this spring, ain't ye? An' mark my word, the harvest is just as sure."

I wish we could think so.

MONDAY, MAY 16

Ed took his boys out for a hike and picnic this evening. The little brothers went along—and seven-year-old Cary Mills was the first to arrive at the parsonage. Scarcely had the clock struck four when he appeared, lunch pail in hand and on his head the precious white sailor hat.

The children had a hilarious time. The boys were hungry after several rounds of playing "Steal the Bacon" and "Last Couple Out." And as they ran for their lunch pails, there was an unexpected collision between Bill and Dale, which brought forth from the younger boy a tirade of abusive language.

"Say, listen, kid," Bill began in measured tones. "If you hafta talk that way, save it till you get home. We don't talk like that here."

"We're making progress, Laurie," Ed said tonight. "Remember last fall when the vocabularies of most of the youngsters were limited to abuse?"

The older boys were solicitous hosts to their little brothers. These last months of living close to the boys, sharing and stretching their interests, has been rewarding for both them and their Gebby.

"Cantcha take us camping all night sometime, Gebby?" Cary pleaded around the dying fire.

"Aw, gee, you oughta take us fer a whole week," begged Warren.

That's quite an order to fill.

FRIDAY, MAY 20

Ed climbed the Gold Valley hill this afternoon to the little house beyond the crossroads, where blind old Grandma Simmons is living alone. When Grandpa Simmons passed away, Ed cautioned her after the funeral, "Don't try to live up here alone, Grandma. At least find a neighbor who can help you out often." Yet sightless, kinless, and nearly friendless, she has clung to the old home with its familiar paths and furnishings.

"Laurie," Ed said when we met at the church, "she hadn't had a pail of fresh water since the day of the funeral, three weeks ago, till I filled her bucket today. And I doubt if the kitchen floor has been swept since then either. Yet she's determined to stay up there."

"Are you going to stop in to see the welfare worker at Gorman?"

"I guess I'll have to—but first I'm telling my scouts."

MONDAY, MAY 23

Tonight we prayed before we went to the Gorman church board meeting that somehow the way for the Gorman church would seem clearer, and that there might be a unity of spirit in place of the divisive discouragement which has so often characterized the group. How completely that prayer was answered!

The board meeting proceeded as usual: church budget low and the building in need of repairs. Ed let things go as they willed. The business meeting limped along to a weak conclusion. Then Mr. Marston, the chairman of the board of trustees, arose.

"I've had a few things on my mind," he began quietly.

"That vesper music before Easter, the brave attempt our youngsters have made to beautify these bare windows, the earnest efforts of our ladies to lay aside for the future of this little church—these things have made me think.

"Listen, friends, this town needs our little church. We wouldn't live here without it. But we've been content with too little. We haven't sacrificed enough. We've aimed too low. And we're failing in the Lord's work in this community. With our lack of space and equipment we can't be a light in this town. We can't have the sort of church gatherings in which fellowship and unity can grow.

"It isn't because our pastor hasn't dreamed and planned," he went on. "He has architect's drawings ready. I admit I haven't given my enthusiastic support to him. And that's what's required. I'm prepared to give that now. I'm going to make a pledge tonight, and I'm going to promise you that I will not stop till every family in our church has been urged to do likewise."

The others were inspired by his earnestness. If only they could know how we have waited and prayed for this change of spirit! They pledged four hundred dollars tonight and appointed committees to begin immediate consideration of our needs and of the architect's plans. We closed the meeting with deeper prayers in our hearts than upon our lips.

PART IV

SUMMER

Behold the fowls of the air: for they sow not, neither do they reap, nor gather into barns; yet your heavenly Father feedeth them. Are ye not much better than they?

Consider the lilies of the field, how they grow; they toil not, neither do they spin: and yet I say unto you, That even Solomon in all his glory was not arrayed like one of these. Wherefore, if God so clothe the grass of the field, which to day is, and to morrow is cast into the oven, shall he not much more clothe you, O ye of little faith?

But seek ye first the kingdom of God, and his right-eousness; and all these things shall be added unto you.
—From Matthew 6

SUNDAY, MAY 29

> *O day of rest and gladness,*
> *O day of joy and light . . .*

This has been a true Sabbath indeed. The snow of bridal wreath upon the hedges, the perfume and lavender of lilacs in the bushes, and tonight the quiet beauty of the Gold Valley church, its windows framing the sunset. How grateful we are for these days.

And some of today's moments of wonder and worship were not spent within the walls of our churches, but beneath the endless blue of summer skies. After the preacher's nap this afternoon we wandered back to the hills north of town, past newly sown fields and along the ridges of sand hills to the Stanton farm.

On the wide veranda of their home, facing their broad fields, we talked of many things. Farmer Stanton showed us maps of his fields and explained how he rotated his crops.

"Maybe I'm wrong," he said, "but I hold it's as sinful fer a man to punish his lands as to punish his horse. The land is the Lord's. I'm jes' His caretaker."

FRIDAY, JUNE 10

Stacked high on the dining-room table are marionette remnants and candle wax molds. Anyone who knows the preacher and his wife might guess that vacation Bible schools are in session. Mornings at Gorman, a hurried lunch, afternoons at Gold Valley, then the leisurely drive home, during which we share the experiences of the day and plan the program for the morrow—such has been the schedule for the week.

"Laurie, why do you suppose the Burton youngsters have been attending every other day?" Ed asked on our way home from Gold Valley yesterday.

"That caught my curiosity too. So I asked Irene. Seems it's a family compromise. Pop Burton says, 'Go to vacation Bible school? Oh, no! You don't get outa helpin' me in the hayfields that easy.' And Ma Burton says, 'If you kids want to go enough to hike five miles in the hot sun, I guess I can take your place in the fields.' "

"I see. So every other day they work with Pop Burton in the hayfields, and every other day we get our turn at them. Some system for settling family differences. Say, Laurie, we're going to bring your fiddle along tomorrow and accept Ben Burton's invitation to call."

So today we found the Burton farm. The sky was an endless blue, hazy at the horizon. Their road is little more than a trail, winding over sand hills, down through a tama-

rack swamp, and past a lake or two. The dusty trail was alive with wild things. Ducks settled down on the lakes, a pheasant scampered across the road ahead of us, a woodchuck slipped from the roadway into a swampy ditch, a blue heron flew out of the tamaracks. Fields of corn, the green spears against the brown earth in regular intervals like the pattern of a calico dress, hugged the roadway up to the house.

The house sits like a lonely gray bird on the brow of a sand hill. It's about the same color as the drifting sand around it. The front porch warned us of the disarray we would find inside. Several large racks, which would hold drying corn later in the summer, were leaning against the wall. Remnants of broken machinery and a few miscellaneous tools lay about. A fat lazy cat slowly slipped out of the hot sun into the shade of a broken porch step.

Mrs. Burton called to me from the garden. "Ben an' the kids are in the hayfields," she said. "We're like a bunch of gypsies in the summer. We live in the garden and the fields. See enough of the four drab walls inside during the long winter."

"You surely have an ambitious garden. It must keep the whole family busy," I remarked.

"We don't have much use for a grocery store. Grow all our food for the year in these rows. Want a bouquet of vegetables? That's the only kind of bouquets I have time for."

She cut several bunches of leafy lettuce, pulled a handful of red radishes, then turned to the pea patch, where the first fat pods burdened the vines.

"While I pick a mess of peas for supper, just go out to the farthest fence post and look out beyond. Guess that's

my church. When I get blue or feel ugly, I just go out there for a while and come back calmed."

I walked over to the edge of the garden and leaned against the fence post. A little lake below mirrored the blue sky, the waving hayfields stretched to the water's edge, and the rest of the lake was belted by a tamarack swamp. Beyond, the wilderness stretched out to reach the horizon. I thought of the psalmist's words: "He leadeth me beside the still waters. He restoreth my soul."

Ed had found Ben Burton in the field below the rough-hewn log barn, and in a little while we saw Leland and Irene on the flats below driving the cows home.

After supper Mrs. Burton and I spent a happy hour at the organ and cello. Her listening family reminded me of thirsty soil drinking in a summer's rain. Soon Mr. Burton

was on his knees near the organ, sorting through a large pile of worn music.

"Here's what I've been wantin' to hear you play while Vera sings," he said at last and put a tattered copy of Schubert's "Ave Maria" on the organ.

When we rose to go, Mr. Burton followed Ed around to the other side of the car.

"Come often," he said. Then he added with frank sincerity, "We like you, and I'm not a man to put into words what your wife's fiddlin' does to me, but your church—I don't know. It hasn't made many saints outa the sinners of this community."

Sunday, June 12

When we arrived on the shores of Diamond Lake for the annual Fairhaven Children's Day program and picnic, the mist we drove in had turned to a summer drizzle. We found our congregation out in the woods under the dripping trees, however, and on the improvised platform at the center of a large semicircle the Children's Day program was in progress. The old organ from the church basement was protected by a large tarpaulin draped about it like a cape, but the organist sat in the rain.

By lunch time the drizzle had become a steady rain, and Mrs. Johnson opened her resort to the congregation, since her guests were away on a fishing trip. However wet the weather may have been, nothing could have dampened the spirits of the group.

"If this was a year ago—or any of the drouth years," said Grandma Webster to me—"we'd have eaten in the rain 'nd thanked God for the privilege."

Friday, June 17

Our home is a bountiful garden tonight—sweet peas from the Bergs, peonies from the Gunters, tiger lilies from the Marstons, and simple little bachelor's buttons from our own back yard. But none are so lovely as the

generous bouquet of wild flowers which the Gorman children presented to us at the vacation Bible school program tonight.

These have been rewarding weeks with the children of our parish. Each morning the preacher has ventured forth in the little parsonage car to pick up children from the country who wait at dusty corners for his "bus."

"Reverend, ye look jes' like the old woman who lived in a shoe when ye drive up to the church and open the car doors. Why, I counted an even dozen this mornin'," old Mr. Gunter remarked to Ed one afternoon.

But another member of the church board stopped the preacher on the street the other day. "Can't see why you gotta wear out yer car an' waste yer gas a-bringin' that mob o' kids in. Course, I won't stop ye, but it looks like perty hopeless business to me."

He should have heard one bright-eyed youngster exclaim this evening, "Wish we could have vacation school all summer, an' a picnic every two weeks!"

The gangly marionettes that the children constructed and dressed as Bible characters are piled high on the preacher's filing cabinet. Tonight at the program the loose-jointed dolls, with boys and girls pulling their strings, interpreted with agility and expression several of the stories which Jesus told.

The preacher and his gang of boys have spent many hours discussing the teachings of the prophets.

"What should we do about the county relief workers who have decided to strike because they don't want to work in the hot sun?" Ed asked one day after they had discussed the teachings of Amos, the prophet of justice.

"Take one of 'em out an' shoot 'im—then the rest would get busy," was Bill's ready solution.

"That's pretty drastic," Ed objected.

The next day they discussed the teachings of Hosea, the prophet of mercy.

"I see whatcha mean," Bill finally assented. "I guess we gotta try to understand the other fella."

"Say, Gebby," put in Warren, "I'll betcha you woulda got awful sore at us kids last winter if you hadn't really cared about us an' tried to understand."

THURSDAY, JUNE 23

A moonlight night on the shore of a quiet lake, a roaring fire, and skeeters enough to keep us active—"This is the life," was the sentiment of everyone in the Fairhaven youth group.

They're likable farm youngsters—the wholesome, dependable sort one longs to believe the world is becoming increasingly full of. Tonight they won us with their confident idealism concerning the ability of young people to build a better world. No skepticism here! Somehow these young people who live near the soil with growing things all about them—from newborn calves and baby chicks to the thin spears of corn that shove their way through the brown earth in geometric intervals—possess a stability, a sureness about the ways of God that many town young people lack.

We discussed the compassion offering we are planning for the hospital.

"Why couldn't we send down fresh garden vegetables and canned goods?" was a suggestion.

"We could," Ed replied. "You grow them and fill my car, and I'll take them down."

"It's a deal," the group chorused.

SATURDAY, JUNE 25

"Say, have I ever got somethin' to show you," shouted Warren as he bounded into the parsonage kitchen this morning. "Guess what?"

"Couldn't. I'm never surprised at anything from you."

"Well, it's got somethin' to do with that scout book."

"Has it? Let's see. Pigeons?" I asked, venturing a wild guess.

"Aw, Mom musta told you. Well, you jes' oughta see 'em. I've got two pair. A brown pair with colored lights all over their wings, an' the prettiest snow white Kings you ever saw. Traded a jackknife an' a nickel fer 'em, then had to climb to the top o' Brown's silo after 'em." Then his tousled head bobbed toward me. "D'you think they'll have babies?"

"If they don't fly away," I laughed.

"Oh, I been a-studyin' up on that. Old man Gunter showed me how to fix a pen fer 'em, an' Pop told me I could use the attic of the garage fer their roost. Says he wouldn't mind a pigeon pie."

"Someday you'll be earning that pigeon merit badge."

"I sure will. An' lots of others, too. Say, when's Gebby gonna take us campin'?"

"Is he?"

"Sure. Mom says you'd better come too to make sure we get enough to eat."

"We'll have to talk to the preacher about that."

When Ed came in from his hospital calls, he had plans. "Let's drive out to the Stanton farm, Laurie. Farmer Stanton bought new a team the other day. Wanted us to come out and see it."

We sought a new trail north of town that led out to the rolling hill country. The fields of heading grain—barley,

87

rye, oats, and wheat—were like waving seas of color. The wild rose bushes in June bloom ran rampant along the roadside and spread into the unkempt edges of the woods. Farmer Stanton was loading hay into the barn and took time out to explain the process to the preacher's wife.

"I'll race you to the top of the stack in the haymow," called out his five-year-old grandson. We played in the hay, and found the baby kittens, and petted the newborn calf.

"Do you know of a good camp site around these hills?" Ed asked at supper time. "My gang of boys from Gorman and the scouts from Gold Valley are plaguing me for a week of camping."

"Even the girls at Gold Valley are begging for it, Ed," I added.

"Say, pastor," Mr. Stanton began slowly, "wouldn't wonder I could help ye. What would ye think of Grandpa Stanton's picnic grove, Martha?"

"Our girls and all their friends used to love that place," his wife said. "It'd sure be grand to have young folks down there agin—if it's good enough."

"You see, this wooded forty runs down to the lake shore, and on the lake is where Grandpa Stanton had his sawmill. Course it's jes' a clearin' now, but the cattle keep the clover clipped, and we think it's perty nice. Let's go down after supper."

So we drove down the pasture trail and into the green twilight of deep woods. Finally we broke out into the sunlight again on the sloping shores of the lake. It was the spot we had been looking for. Mr. Stanton's face beamed when he saw our delight.

"Why, pastor, nothin' could give Martha an' me more joy than havin' a batch o' kids down here in the woods.

We miss our own mightily. You'd be fillin' an awful big empty spot by bringin' 'em."

Now our children can go camping "fer a whole week." I wonder who is more excited, Gebby or his gang.

SATURDAY, JULY 12

Sometimes I think there is no happier hour each week in the parsonage than that hour on Saturday evenings when the preacher asks, "Laurie, would you like to hear my sermon for tomorrow?" And I listen, relaxed and responsive, as he checks through the service for the morrow. All week he has been gleaning from his study and his experience among our people materials which will bring guidance and strength to our flock on Sunday morning. And then comes Saturday, the day set apart for work and worship in the parsonage study. Sometimes it is a day of whims— perhaps a picnic supper on some lonely lake shore or pancakes and bacon for lunch, perhaps cello music or a plate of fudge at bedtime. Always it is a day that I reserve for the preacher's requirements.

Then in the evening hour as I listen to the fruit of the day's labor, I await my share in the creation—perhaps an apt illustration or a long-sought word, perhaps a hymn for the order of worship that sings the message of the sermon. On Saturday evenings I always feel a tide of gratefulness that the preacher's tasks are our tasks—"shared," as the Prophet says, "with joy that is unacclaimed."

WEDNESDAY, JULY 6

"Can we really go camping fer a whole week, an' sleep in tents, an' eat outdoors? Gee whiz, that'll be swell." I can still hear the eager cries.

About fifteen boys from Gorman and Gold Valley were gathered on the parsonage front steps planning one of the greatest thrills of their young lives. Ed told them about the Stanton woods and shore line, and their eyes sparkled. Fishing, swimming, scouting, and all you want to eat—what more could be needed to complete a boy's dream of heaven?

The boys decided if they brought enough garden vegetables and groceries from home, they could manage their camping trip on a quarter a week, which would be enough for fresh milk. That means both of the Omann boys can go, and not even Dan Mead from Gold Valley will have to stay home from the week's camping trip because of lack of funds.

SATURDAY, JULY 9

Tonight at sunset we went on a treasure hunt, down the highway and along the tracks. I think our very first treasure was that gold-orange sky in the west, which wrapped our humble little village in its glamorous haze, and the banks of silver clouds, gold-lined. And then there were flowers, seas of them, in such riotous colors as only nature can create and intermingle. I brought home a bouquet of grasses with just enough flower color to set off the fuzzy-wigs and the long, graceful sticklers.

God of growing things, God of life, we thank Thee that, as the grasses and flowers reveal Thee to us, our lives may reveal Thee to others. We thank Thee that, as the grain heads and comes to fruitfulness, so do the lives of Thy children. Give us Thy patience, O God. Help us to trust Thy quiet miracle of growth, that we may guide young lives to Thee, and be led to Thee through them.

TUESDAY, JULY 12

Take a peek into my kitchen! It's a shady spot beneath a canopy of trees. The old oil stove and a camp gasoline stove share the plank between two sawhorses. Both stoves have been busy today, for camping or not, the parsonage winter supply of cherries had to be canned. The younger boys caught on to this canning spree and by noon brought in a milk pail full of gooseberries—some of them the prickly variety—from the clearing beyond the woods.

I've fried fish every meal so far. Ed chooses new fishermen each day, and they row out to the edge of the water reeds to drop their lines. In half an hour they come dashing over

the rocks and the clover clearing to the kitchen canopy with their string of crappies and sunfish and excited stories about the "big one that got away."

Each night at campfire time I've mixed up biscuit batter for bread sticks. The boys are good campfire cooks. They

bake and brown the bread sticks, slip the tender biscuit from the stick, and fill the hole with jelly or a slice of cheese. I used eight cups of flour and a pound of lard last night before the gang stopped calling for more batter.

Wednesday, July 13

A bee tree provided today's excitement. The morning chore crew found it while they were scouting through the woods for campfire timber. There it stood—a hollow stump about twelve feet high, with an occasional bee soaring above. Warren and Dan Mead set to work feverishly chopping the old stump down. Then the bees found the boys. It took all of us and a smudge or two before the bees were placated and the honey retrieved. Dan carries his arm limply tonight, and Warren sits down with peculiar care, but when the bread sticks were filled with honey, the boys agreed their dearly bought treasure was worth the stings.

Thursday, July 14

I wonder what Farmer Stanton's cows think when they find their favorite pastures usurped by rustic bridges and lean-tos, roughhewn tables and chairs, constructed in pioneer style. The boys and the cattle quarreled this afternoon over which would occupy the swimming hole.

Yesterday when the Omann boys went forth, armed with a spade, to dig a new and deeper garbage hole, they found almost perfect modeling clay under the rich topsoil of the woods, and we have spent hours since modeling everything from fish to pottery out of God's good earth.

Mealtimes are hilarious. Two twelve-foot planks on sawhorses make our table, and the bench on either side is another plank set on good-sized stumps. This morning the

boys raced to see who could consume the most pancakes. The griddle and cook were both hot and busy. Tonight we listened to tall stories as Dan Mead and Bill Adams vied to see which could spin the most outlandish yarn.

Each evening at twilight we've gathered around the blazing campfire, but tonight after supper chores were done, Warren and Jack called us all to the lake shore to watch the sun set behind the black pillars of a thundercloud. The lake was aflame with the reflected colors of the sky. A pair of loons circled above us, and the stillness was broken only by their eerie cry.

"Gee, but the sky's pretty," Warren said quietly. "Makes you think God's a great artist to paint a sky like that, don't it, Gebby?"

FRIDAY, JULY 15

Several times when Ed and I have settled down in our tent at night with only the tree toads and crickets to listen in, we have said to each other, "Our boys have come a long, long way." And tonight around our last campfire I thought again of our first outing with the gang, when, because of their bickering, quarrelsome mood, each one built his own fire and ate his lunch alone.

Tonight there were wieners in the bread sticks—a special treat from Warren's uncle. As twilight deepened into dark, we sang all the songs we had learned this week. Then after Gebby's story we stood in our last friendship circle and sang "Lord, I Want to Be a Christian in My Heart."

SATURDAY, JULY 23

I wore the preacher's whistle this week—and watched the dreams of a dozen little girls come true. The Gold Val-

ley Girl Scouts filled the five tents in the Stanton woods, and Evelyn and I hiked, swam, fished, studied, worshiped, and played with them. Each afternoon nature contrived with us to give them a rest period. A thundershower came up during nap time, so we dug trenches about the tents, fastened them securely, and shooed our wards to bed till the sun came out from behind the thunderheads.

There were the hushed evenings around the campfire, when in the dusk of the woods we worshiped and prayed together.

I think I shall always remember Mary Mead. She was as carefree as a little songbird all the day long. In the evenings when we were back in our tents, it was hard sometimes for the girls to quiet down and go to sleep. Several nights I noticed that while the other girls were whispering to each other, Mary too was talking quietly—but to herself. One night I listened. And I was surprised. Mary, from as sordid and liquor-soaked a home as there is in bedraggled Gold Valley, was repeating to herself one lovely prayer and bit of scripture after another. I heard the Shepherd's Psalm, the Lord's Prayer, snatches of shorter verses, and finally, as the tired, glad girl was falling asleep, I heard, "Thank You, God, for these happy days."

"The kingdom of heaven is like to a grain of mustard seed."

WEDNESDAY, AUGUST 3

Across the town comes the humdrum tune of the county fair merry-go-round. We didn't allow ourselves even to be tempted by the fair; but tonight, when the evening air was full of cooling wind and rain, we strolled around the block and had a short swing in the park.

"Are you going to help me can blueberries tomorrow?"
I asked the preacher.

"Blueberries?"

"Yes. We had a little visitor today. And he came laden
with blueberries."

"The Millses are back from their summer trek to the
border?"

"Yes, and Cary came to call. He brought his little wagon
full of berries. He wants us to come over and watch the
men put in the foundation for their new home tomorrow
morning. They're building out near the fair grounds.
'Mom says we get a new house 'cause I was such a good
berrypicker,' he said. He surely was a proud little boy."

"Say, I saw them digging that basement when I came
home today. That's just a block or two across the fields
from the parsonage."

"It's going to mean a lot to them to get away from the
alley back of Norb's Place, isn't it?"

"Yes, Laurie, especially if they can leave some of their
old companions behind too."

FRIDAY, AUGUST 5

The trains on the branch line that runs through Gold
Valley have a new stop. Every train, whether it is a long
chain of empty freight cars, a string of oil tankers, or the
daily mail-and-passenger coach, stops at Gold Valley now.
The crew and an occasional passenger climb out and bound
into the station rooms to listen to the rich chiming of
Dad Houston's two clocks and measure his progress on the
present masterpiece. He has the clocks set so that the music
of the chimes is almost constant.

"What'll I take fer 'em?" Dad Houston asked incredulously of a prospective buyer. "Why, mister, they ain't fer sale—not as long as I'm here to enjoy 'em myself."

MONDAY, AUGUST 8

Imagine playing Santa Claus in midsummer! We spent the morning and a part of the afternoon gathering vegetables for the hospital. We stopped at one farm after another where heaping bushels of tomatoes, bulging sacks of cabbages, bunches of beets, and bags of onions were waiting for us. When we crawled back into the car after our last stop at the Websters', I wondered where I was going to sit. There were cabbages packed about our heads, sacks of potatoes and bunches of carrots on the floor under our feet, and a sack of tomatoes between us.

Even my hands were full. Just as we left, prim little Louise came up to the car. She thrust a small candy sack with a few sweet peas sticking through the top into my hands.

"Mrs. Gebhard," she said in a precise little voice, "will you please give this to some little sick girl? It isn't very

much, but there wasn't much ripe in my garden. Just three ground cherries and two yellow tomatoes. You take them for me."

WEDNESDAY, AUGUST 10

Mr. Gunter will serve on the building committee.

Men of the Fairhaven church will give two days' volunteer work to help with the excavation.

Farmer Kleinbacher will lend team of horses for excavating.

Ernie Mills has offered the use of his truck.

Boy Scouts plan to set out trees on boulevard.

Anonymous gift of five hundred dollars pledged to pastor.

So runs the list of notations that the preacher has scribbled off for the Gorman building committee meeting tonight.

"Son," Mr. Gunter remarked to Ed a few minutes ago, "I'll be the first one on the job Monday morning to begin with the excavatin'. An' when ye start pourin' the cement, I want to manage the mixin'. Why, boy, my dreams is a-comin' true!"

And as the congregation has gathered about the drawings on the east church wall, we have heard the same remark many times. The precise sketches show the new addition, a large square room with basement underneath, built at a right angle to the present structure and joined by a spacious belfry tower.

"An' where the old doorway is," said Mr. Gunter when the committee studied the plans, "there orta be a window— a large stained-glass window with the same warm sunset colors the young folks has got in them others."

THURSDAY, AUGUST 11

As we drove home from Fairhaven this afternoon, we slowed down on the open highway just outside of town. There, hugging the roadside, were the charred ruins of a burned truck.

"Someone's living gone up in flames," Ed said as we drove by.

"Ed, that looked like the Millses' truck."

"Sure enough, it did. Let's drop around past the new house when we get to town."

Our fears were soon confirmed. The dejected little family were sitting on their porch as we stopped, looking as though the world were going to end. Fortunately there was no load in the truck, and the loss was partially covered by insurance.

"This is a fine time fer a man to lose his means o' livin', ain't it, preacher?" Mr. Mills asked bitterly.

"Listen, man," Ed told him, "you aren't licked while you've got your strength and something to work for."

"I guess I ain't," he said, a flicker of a smile on his face. "Guess I have seen it tougher 'n this."

FRIDAY, AUGUST 19

We drove out the Burton way before the Gold Valley Sunshine Club meeting this afternoon. Ben was mending the pasture fence, and Ed walked across the fields to visit with him while he worked.

"Say, preacher," Mr. Burton said, "it's none o' my business, but I've almost decided those church folks o' yours don't care much about their church. That buildin's been needin' paint fer years, an' every passin' season don't

help much. Now, I'm a carpenter by trade, an' I don't like t' see a good buildin' like that goin' t' rot 'cause o' the weather."

"I've been waiting all year to hear someone say that to me," Ed replied.

"Well, I jes' want you to know that, come fall, I'll match the days of volunteer labor any other man's willin' to give to help paint the church."

"Will you match the preacher's?"

"Sure will. In fact, I wouldn't mind workin' along side the preacher."

"Well, we may let you boss the job," Ed assured him.

We drove into Gold Valley and stepped into the Sunshine Club meeting.

"Umph, I guess I don't have to 'pologize to any man fer my paintin'," seventy-year-old Grandma Jarvis was saying. "Course," she added, "I wouldn't be very good up on a ladder."

"The ladies are a-gonna paint the church fer you, preacher," Ma Thompson, the chairman, explained to us.

"Good," Ed replied. "What are you going to paint it with?"

"Oh, we've got that all settled. Ma Thompson and Grandma Jarvis have been soliciting in town this week. They collected a quarter here, fifty cents there," said Mrs. Houston.

"We've got twenty dollars already," said Ma Thompson.

"An' we're a-goin' out to the country homes this week an' git the balance!" added Grandma Jarvis.

"Why, some of the men have even promised to come an' help us paint," said Ma Thompson.

"Yes," put in the preacher, "I found a foreman to boss the job this afternoon."

"Who told you what was a-goin' on here this afternoon?" teased Ma Thompson.

"You'll be glad for a little masculine help before you get through with the church tower," Ed countered.

Perhaps soon we won't need to feel ashamed of the drab, neglected appearance of the little church on Gold Valley's main street.

Tuesday, August 23

I had just arranged an armful of scarlet and white gladiolas from the Gunter garden this afternoon when there was a knock at the door. It was Mrs. Mills. She looked troubled.

"How's the new house, neighbor?" I asked as pleasantly as I could.

"Mrs. Gebhard, we're in trouble again. I just stopped by to see if Reverend could help us."

"What is it?" I asked.

"It's Ernie this time. He's been terribly discouraged ever since the truck burned. But now it's his eyes. Since he started working on the interior of the house, they've been bothering him. They're red and sore, and this morning he had trouble seeing out of the right eye at all."

"Has he been to the doctor?"

"Yes, he was up this morning. I don't know what the doctor told him. But from the way Ernie's been acting, I'm afraid. The truck's gone. Ernie's eyes pain him terribly. I don't know how we'll manage. The savings from this summer that we had laid up for the house will have to go to keep us in food now, I guess."

"Don't worry," I told her. "There's a way out somehow. I'll ask Ed to stop in to see Ernie."

"I wish you would. He feels awfully discouraged. The
100

doctor's ordered him to live in a dark room and keep quiet for a while. That's hard for a man like him."

WEDNESDAY, AUGUST 31

Our solicitous milkman stopped this morning for more than his customary greeting.

"Say, you folks know the Millses, don'tcha?" he asked. "Well, jes' wanted you to know that they've canceled their milk order. She said somethin' about hatin' to do it, 'cause of the boy, but they jes' can't keep up with the milk tickets since Mr. Mills went blind. Poor man's havin' a painful time of it, I guess. Course," he said as he left the porch step, "I been leavin' a quart on the doorstep now an' then anyhow."

Ed went down to the new little house across the fields this afternoon. Mrs. Mills led him into the dark bedroom where Mr. Mills, a crumpled, discouraged man, was sitting.

"Reverend," he began desperately, "why is it? Jes' when I thought at last I could begin to give Cary and Mina what they deserve. I jes' can't take it. A big strong man like me—blind."

"What does the doctor say, Ernie?" Ed asked gently.

"I don't know," he replied. "I think he knows more 'n he says. I'm afraid he doesn't have much hope. Sometimes I think the kid 'nd 'is mother could make out better 'thout me. These eyes—I could tear 'em out at times, they ache so."

Ed stopped in the kitchen to visit with Mrs. Mills.

"He's just getting worse and worse," she said frantically. "The sight in one eye is gone, and the other is failing rapidly. If only the doctor could do something!"

Later this afternoon Ed met Dr. MacGregor on the street.

"I'm concerned about that man," the doctor said. "He's

101

lost hope, and really there isn't much chance for saving his
eyesight either. Perhaps the specialist at Middleton could
help him out. I'd like to have him look at those eyes anyway."

THURSDAY, SEPTEMBER 1

Industry is afoot at the church corner in Gorman. The
rhythmic chug of the cement mixer and the thud of the
carpenter's hammer have become as familiar as the inter-
mittent call of the meadow lark and the steady hum of
traffic on the highway. I just carried home a tray of twelve
empty lemonade glasses and a platter with one lone dough-
nut left on it. Ed and Bill were pouring cement for the
basement; young Warren and one of the Omann boys
were digging a place in the far corner for the furnace. Mr.
Gunter stood next to the cement mixer directing the work
of Bob Omann and Jack Adams.

"Guess I ain't so spry any more," he remarked when I
offered him his lemonade. "Most I kin do now is order
these boys about. Say, missis," he added quietly, "I was jes'
a-tellin' the Reverend that when this job's all done, I got
some shrubs and bulbs over home that'd make a mighty
perty little garden there where the walk is now."

"In front of your stained-glass window?" I asked, as he
pointed to the sagging old doorway. He nodded approv-
ingly.

PART V

AUTUMN

For every tree is known by his own fruit. For of thorns men do not gather figs, nor of a bramble bush gather they grapes. A good man out of the good treasure of his heart bringeth forth that which is good; and an evil man out of the evil treasure of his heart bringeth forth that which is evil: for of the abundance of the heart his mouth speaketh.

—Luke 6:44-45

But the fruit of the Spirit is love, joy, peace, long-suffering, gentleness, goodness, faith, meekness, temperance: against such there is no law.

—Gal. 5:22-23

TUESDAY, SEPTEMBER 6

There's the scarlet of woodbine against the gray-green hills now, and the crimson ivy twines in and out of the grasses at the road's edges. Last night's frost nipped the cornfields, and only the hardy perennials are left blooming in the Gunter's garden.

"When the sumac starts to turn 'nd the ducks go south, it's 'bout time we got in the church's wood supply," Grandpa Webster said outside the Fairhaven church last Sunday. So today we helped with the Fairhaven wood bee. The men of the congregation hauled the winter's fuel supply from the woods and buzzed it up into furnace lengths.

"Jes' you bring yer trailer along, pastor, 'n we'll give

103

ye a good start on your winter's fuel too," Grandpa Webster said.

While the saw buzzed behind the church, the women prepared a country dinner in the church kitchen.

"Know what? The church has a birthday next month," said Alice Webster. "We ought to celebrate."

"Ten years since this building was finished! That does call for a celebration."

"We ought to make it a big party!"

"And bring our birthday pennies?"

"Sure—to pay off the church debt."

That's a brave undertaking, for in the nine years of drought that succeeded the church's erection, the faithful congregation has scarcely been able to pay the interest, much less attempt to reduce the principal of the church debt. But crops have been good this season, and when the Fairhaven farmers prosper, so does the church they love.

The enthusiasm spread. By the time the men came in for dinner, there was a harvest of ideas, and committees were soon appointed. The preacher and his wife were asked to help plan the program. We'll have to put on our thinking caps to find something worthy of the occasion.

WEDNESDAY, SEPTEMBER 7

It's been a cold, cheerless day. The wind has ridden through town, stripping our trees. The preacher just returned from taking Ernie Mills to Middleton, where the specialist looked at his eyes. He gave Ernie a thread of hope. How the suffering man clings to it! The doctor is ready to operate to save the sight of the left eye, but he's not sure that the right eye will ever see again. He warned Ernie it would be a difficult, painful operation, and there would

still be many weeks of darkness ahead. Yet how Ernie looks forward to this chance for sight!

Mrs. Mills spent a part of the afternoon with me. The Gorman Ladies' Aid has been buying milk for little Cary. Mrs. Mills seemed most appreciative, though, of the visitors from the church. "They've brought such friendliness," she said, "that no matter what happens, we don't feel as though we're standing alone."

"And you aren't," I assured her.

THURSDAY, SEPTEMBER 8

The preacher's joints were stiff when he awoke this morning. "Too much cement totin'," I said.

"Just shows I need a little more instead of less of it, Laurie. At least I have the satisfaction of knowing that the Gorman church has a solid foundation."

This afternoon after my last batch of tomatoes was in the canner, I walked over to the church to watch the carpenters put up the heavy beams for the addition. Mr. Gunter was watching too.

"Had a visitor here a while ago."

"Yes?"

"Chairman o' the trustees. Says the money's 'bout all in."

"That'll make Ed rejoice."

"I dunno. He warn't quite sure it were rightful fer us t'allow our preacher to haul cement an' help the carpenters. Was afraid the town folks might talk."

"Did you tell him he'd have a job keeping Gebby out of such excitement?"

"Nope. I jes' says, 'Tell them folks what ain't seen a preacher in overalls before that the Master o' men was a carpenter.' "

FRIDAY, SEPTEMBER 9

This afternoon before our Gold Valley scout meetings Ed and I stopped at the empty store building where Evelyn Hughes has opened the community recreation center. It is empty no longer. The discarded showcases and shelves have been pressed into service to display the products of the handcraft classes. At the long counters women were making glass paintings, spattering luncheon cloths; children were modeling in clay and carving in soap. A couple of old men sat in the far corner whittling at diamond willow sticks.

"Even Dad Houston's going to help us," Evelyn told us. "Guess he doesn't think the town's quite so hopeless as he used to. Seemed to be just waiting for a chance to help the boys with their coping-saw designs. He even said he thought we were doing 'a whale of a job keepin' the younguns outa mischief.'"

"We knew he'd come around," I answered.

"Well, some sorta think the whole town has. At least folks is a-comin' round t' different sorta things than they usta," Ma Thompson put in, looking up from her glass painting.

At one end of the long room were ping-pong tables and indoor golf. A knot of boys and girls were gathered about them. It seemed to us that Evelyn had gleaned skills and ideas from all over, had mastered them herself, and then had taught them to the community.

As I looked into Evelyn's smiling face, there flashed through my mind the thoughtful, confused look Doris, her sister, had had months ago; and her words echoed, "If only I'd had a chance like Evelyn!"

"We're having our final kitten-ball game after school,"

106

Evelyn told us. "Better stop over at the lot and watch the town gang play the country kids." ·

WEDNESDAY, SEPTEMBER 14

"I don't know whether you were painting the church or painting yourself," Ed said, looking at my paint-

besmeared slacks as we backed across the street to appraise the results of our day's labor in Gold Valley.

"I had a good time anyway." Then I turned to watch the sun glistening on the newly painted walls of the church.

"Thompsons are planning to paint their store now—think the church shows it up too much."

"And it looks as though Mr. Hughes is preparing for a paint job too."

"Yes, Laurie, and Mrs. Morris asked me today if I didn't think the schoolhouse could stand a coat of paint. I didn't discourage her."

"And little Mary Mead came dashing over to the church at noon. 'Guess what!' she cried, 'Ma's whitewashin' our house!'"

First thing we know the whole town will have a fresh, clean face because the church was painted.

Thursday, September 15

The sunsets of autumn have settled down over the hills and woods of our north country. The tawny gold of the goldenrod and the lavender of the little clumps of wild asters are the only spots of color left in the fields and along the roadways.

The preacher spent the day with Mr. and Mrs. Mills at the Middleton Hospital. Ed and Mrs. Mills returned an hour ago, apprehensive about the success of the operation.

"I'll feel it's a miracle if Ernie ever sees again," Mrs. Mills said wearily as she stepped out of the car.

Little Cary has been my entertaining guest today. He has spent hours with Gebby's homemade puzzles and marble games. Warren and Bill stopped by after school long enough to show him all the wonders of the game box.

Friday, September 16

I climbed the steps to Grandma Jarvis' apartment on the Gold Valley main street this afternoon to admire her windowful of flowers and cheer her a bit in her illness. She is wretched that, after working so hard to prepare for the painting, she has not been well enough to apply even a brushful. Her rocking chair was pulled up in front of the window.

"I been sittin' here all day," she said to me, "a-watchin' yer husband an' Ben Burton climbin' around in the high

belfry of the church. Why, it's been plain excitin'. I guess all the other men in town shied offa gittin' up there."

"Yes," I replied. "Ben and the preacher found a good share of the tower had never been painted, and I guess they're finding out why, too."

"Well, if a man kin git there, Ben'll do it," she said. "Seems queer, him a-paintin' the church. So many years he'd niver go near it. An' niver let his kids go, neither. An' there he is, a-paintin' up there with the preacher!"

"They've had a good time working up there. Ben's a steady workman, and he and Ed have had their share of painting on the top third of the building."

As we drove out to the Burtons' for supper this afternoon, the white paint shone like fresh snow on a cold winter day.

"Well, Ed," I remarked, "there's the reward of your labors."

"No, Laurie, the clean, white church is only one reward. Another was the way Ben Burton said to me today, 'Well, it's our church, ain't it?'"

At choir practice tonight Ben interrupted between the verses of "Fairest Lord Jesus."

"Preacher," he said, "it jes' came t' me. When this paintin' job's done, we gotta celebrate. We gotta have a little music. Like when we git the harvest in at home, we spend the evenin' jes' singin'."

"A Harvest Home Vesper!" Ed exclaimed.

"That's it! At sunset time—in candlelight."

WEDNESDAY, SEPTEMBER 21

A tiny shivery sliver of a new moon hung in the west tonight. Ed and I just came in from a brisk walk around

the church corner, where we paused to measure the progress on the new addition.

There we met Ernie Mills and his little son, out for a daily airing. Ernie must live in the dark for a week or so longer, so father and son go walking in the cool, quiet light of the early evening. Ernie is more hopeful than ever that the doctor's patient skill has worked a miracle.

"My boy's a great pal," he said as we stopped to visit with them. "Never knew Cary could mean so much to me as he's meant durin' these long weeks."

Sunday, September 25

"Pastor, you gotta help us out," said Ken Webster when we arrived for the Fairhaven service this morning. "It's the same old argument every Temperance Sunday. In the Adult Bible Class we spend the hour a-hecklin' between the farmers and the tourist resort owners. The farmers point a finger of shame at the resort folks 'cause of all the drinkin' that goes on in the cottages, an' the resort owners say, 'Kin we help it? We don't sell the stuff. They bring it in with them. But you farmers don't have to grow malt barley jes' 'cause the price is better.' "

Saturday, October 1

There's a great blue night sky overhead, and the quarter moon is hanging in the western horizon—like a babe's cradle.

We have just had a homey supper of pancakes and syrup at the Wilson home. Warren, proud as a new father, took us out to the woodshed and showed us a shivering, naked, newborn pigeon.

"See? What'd I tell you? There's gonna be lots more, too,

and I've got some new kinds. I'm a-gonna raise the best pigeons in town!"

FRIDAY, OCTOBER 7

Before our Gold Valley scout meetings this afternoon we climbed the hill to blind Grandma Simmons' cottage. She met us at the door and asked us in. Her face was filled with composure and peace.

"Still living alone?" Ed questioned as he looked around the orderly room.

"Yah, yah," she laughed. "Old birds don't find new nests easy. Some kids has adopted me, preacher, 'er I warrant I couldn't a-managed. Little Mary Mead—you know, Ken Mead's youngun—hain't missed hardly a day all summer but what she's here to dust an' sweep an' put me things aright. Then the Thompson boys has been a totin' water in every other day or so an' keepin' the wood bin full. Wonder sometimes if they know what their help an' laughter does to an old woman."

Then we stopped at Dad Houston's familiar workshop, just to listen to the chiming clocks. Dad Houston has nearly finished another walnut masterpiece. There are over three thousand pieces of inlaid wood in its elaborate patterns. A spray of flowers fills the center panel. Delicate branches intertwine up the side panels, like traceries of twigs against the darkening skies.

Ed picked up a paper of sketches from Dad Houston's workbench. "Another clock?" he asked.

"Wal," Dad Houston drawled, "now that ye asked, I'll have t' tell ye. Yep, I'm a-gonna start it as soon as I kin git me hands on wood that's nice enough fer a pattern like that. That's the one I'm a-making fer you."

"For me?"

"Yep, preacher, you've earned it. Ain't you kept me at 'em, son?" Then he added confidentially, "Nobody else loves 'em like us."

THURSDAY, OCTOBER 13

The other day when we called at the Johnson resort on Diamond Lake, we found Mrs. Johnson sorting through a box of wool rags that a friend had sent her.

"For my rugs," she explained. "I spend a good many hours after huntin' season hookin' 'em."

She motioned to the rug frame in the next room. The rug on it was heavier and firmer than any I had ever seen, and the pattern attracted me. It was an unusual floral design, worked in deep, rich colors.

"Where do you find patterns like that?" I asked her.

"Oh, I sketch 'em myself. The thing I like about rugs is they don't cost me anything t' do. Pa saves me the heavy gunny sacks, summer customers and friends give me the rags, and even my hook is just an old nail I filed down till I had a hook, an' Pa fixed a handle fer it."

"Ed, I've got an idea for the Fairhaven church birthday party!" I exclaimed. "Why not a hobby show? We've found so many interesting things like these rugs that folks all around save to fill the long winter months with. Old Grandpa Morris in Gold Valley was sharpening his whittling knife when we stopped there."

"Have you seen Grandma Webster's quilts?" Mrs. Johnson asked. "Don't leave them out."

"And Dad Houston's coping-saw cupboards."

"Our oldest boy has a whole shelf of Indian relics—

112

hatchets, arrowheads, and such that he's found around here on the place," she said.

We spent today rounding up hobbies for the party next week. At the service station on the lake road we robbed Oscar Schmidt of diamond willow canes, pillow tops, and crocheted table cloths. He offered us his pet monkeys too, but since Pat, the large one, perched on the station sign last Tuesday and refused to budge till Mr. Schmidt hoisted a ladder and shooed him down, we were fearful that they might not behave. At Larson's we discovered an unusual array of old photographs. We ran down picture collections and crocheted carpets and carried off half the wood-working accomplishments from Dad Houston's workshop. There will be collections of quilts, clay modeling, stuffed game birds, and exquisite wood carvings.

"It's jes' whittlin'," old Grandpa Morris said when we asked for his lifelike wood model of a leaping deer.

MONDAY, OCTOBER 17

When Ed came in about six, he brought visitors, Cary and his dad. What a transformation in a man! Ernie can see. After weeks of depression and discouragement he's excited, eager, just big-boyishly happy over regaining his sight. He's only a shadow of his former broad self. But he can *see* with two eyes, and the fresh eagerness in his speech and attitude gave vigor to us all.

Ed brought them over to lend them patterns and tools to make some game boards. Time hangs heavily on Ernie's hands, and already Cary is a faithful devotee of Chinese checkers and African wari.

"That's somethin' we kin do together," Ernie said, "an' so we'll make our own boards."

FRIDAY, OCTOBER 21

> *Joyful, joyful, we adore Thee,*
>   *God of glory, Lord of love;*
> *Hearts unfold like flow'rs before Thee,*
>   *Opening to the sun above.*

So joyously did these words resound in the little Gold Valley church tonight that, as I looked into the faces of the singing choir, I felt I saw hearts unfolding.

We're practicing for our Harvest Home Vesper. Just when the fields are full of corn shocks and the barns and silos are bulging, when fruit cellars are well filled and piles of pumpkins and squash line the back porches of the farmhouses, our little choir sings of fruitfulness and winter's preparation.

Tonight Ben Burton slipped from his customary seat in the rear of the room to the empty chair beside Leland and lent a rich bass to strains of

> "Come, ye thankful people, come.
> Raise the song of harvest home."

MONDAY, OCTOBER 24

When the great orange ball set behind our little church tonight, we were in the garden gathering the last fruits of the summer's growth. Mrs. Gunter called to us from her back porch. Her voice was tired and tense.

"Pa's ailin'," she said. "He'd like mighty well to have you come over fer a while."

Ed left the pumpkins and squash to me and cut across the back of our garden to our neighbors' little home. He came in just a few minutes ago, his head bowed.

"Well, Laurie," he said as I looked up inquiringly, "I'm afraid our old friend will never see the church completed."

"You mean . . ."

"He hasn't many more days left. He seems, too, to feel that the end is near. We had a wonderful fellowship together. His passing will be as serene and quiet as his whole life has been. Laurie, 'the fruit of the Spirit is love, joy, peace, longsuffering, gentleness, goodness—' "

" 'Faith, meekness, temperance,' " I finished.

"And even now he hasn't forgotten the little church he has so loved." A smile passed over Ed's face. "He kept giving me instructions about all the little details that mean so much to him."

"The little flower garden in front of the stained-glass window?"

"Yes," Ed answered in a whisper, "that's what he spoke of just before I left. 'Maybe it kin be a memorial window now, son,' he said."

WEDNESDAY, OCTOBER 26

"Say, ain'tcha ever gonna make fudge again?" Warren asked as he bounded into the parsonage kitchen after supper. "See here?" His pockets were bulging. "Bill 'n me found a mess o' butternuts out in Gorman Grove. Won'tcha make some fudge?" he teased.

"If you'll crack them and pick them."

"Oh, I'll do that. I'll even beat up the candy when it's cool."

"And eat it up too, I'll bet. You'll have to save enough for Gebby, though. He's got a fudge appetite like yours."

When Warren finished his task on the chopping block in the cellar, he hung over the fudge kettle.

"Say, Mrs. Gebby," he said after some minutes, "d'you hafta study hard to be a preacher?"

"Why?" I asked, trying to be as serious as he.

" 'Cause—well, me an' Bill was talkin' this afternoon."

"Don't tell me Bill wants to be a preacher."

"No—not him. But we was a-thinkin'. No one was much interested in us kids till Gebby came along. And now it's swell."

"Gebby enjoys your gang too, Warren."

"Well, I was a-thinkin'—if bein' a preacher means doin' things like Gebby . . ."

"Why don't you talk to him about it sometime, Warren?"

"Aw, he'd think I was jokin'. Anyhow, that fudge's ready." And so it was.

THURSDAY, OCTOBER 27

Happy birthday to you,
Happy birthday to you.

It's been a joyous evening at Fairhaven, one worthy of remembrance. The hobby exhibit attracted more attention than a side show at the county fair. Then we had a little surprise for the group. We showed a set of stereopticon slides in color, "He That Soweth Good Seed." From the picture of the friendly cow to the scenes of moonlight over the snowbound lake, there was a real message for country families that made them walk from the room a little straighter than they came in.

The triumph of the evening, however, was unplanned. Martha Stanton's large, three-tiered birthday cake, replete with ten lighted candles, covered the small square table. When it was placed in the center of the room, it looked

116

like a glowing centerpiece on a huge banquet board. When we were ready to pass the offering plate for birthday pennies just before cutting the cake, Farmer Stanton stood up and cleared his throat.

"Say, folks, I been a-thinkin' about this debt here," he said. "I understand one member of the church intends tonight to turn over a hundred-dollar note he holds against the property. That's a wonderful expression of loyalty, and we'd all like to equal it. Few of us can. I don't have much ready cash now, but I'm a-gonna have some calves pretty soon. Those calves are a-gonna bring some money. I don't know how much. But I kin dedicate a calf to the Lord's house, 'n some o' you could too. I suggest, pastor, that before the plate is passed, some pieces of paper be passed around, an' if anyone else wants to join me in settin' aside a calf, er a hog, er anything else offen his farm fer use against the church debt, he kin say so on the paper an' pass it in as part of his offering."

Every farmer in the room had listened intently. And the idea took. I was amused, however, when my eyes fell on little Louise Webster. She studied Mr. Stanton as he spoke, and when the white slips of paper were handed out, she reached eagerly for one. I saw her streak across the basement to her mother's side and watched her mother quietly remonstrate with her.

The offering was taken; the cake was cut. At the conclusion of the evening the church treasurer announced the extent of the offering: sixty-one dollars in cash, one one-hundred-dollar note, eleven calves, two hogs, and one big fat hen. Spontaneously the congregation, stirred by the gifts, arose and began singing with power and sincerity, "Praise God, from whom all blessings flow."

SUNDAY, OCTOBER 30

Today was truly God-given. And our joy came from little Gold Valley. At the twilight hour when the Gold Valley church windows framed the last deep colors of the sunset, the little church filled with humble worshipers. Outside the bare, black branches of the trees beyond the west windows were etched against the deep hues of the twilight sky. Inside warm candle flames lit the natural wood altar. Dad Houston brought two tall lilies in glorious bloom for the altar and the organ.

But Ben Burton brought the most beautiful gift of all—two hand-carved candelabra for the rustic altar table. The central candleholder with its taper was straight, and the graceful, curving arms on either side held their glowing candles too. They had been enameled till they rivaled the white of the lilies and glistened in the candlelight.

"Jes' a little whittlin' I did this fall," Ben said as he brought them in.

It was hard to leave the beauty of the setting tonight after the quiet fellowship at the communion table. The Burtons found it so too. Ben came up to Ed while the candles still glowed on the altar.

"Preacher," he said, pointing to the candelabra, "I made 'em fer you. Take 'em with you wherever you go, an' use 'em as you've used 'em tonight. They're yours 'cause you know how to use that sort of thing." Then he added sincerely, "I was jes' tellin' Vera the other day that you folks here in the church have given our boy an' girl some of the richest times they'll ever know. This town owes you and your church a lot—an' so do we."

Little Mary Mead lingered too. "Isn't it pretty here?" she asked, her wide eyes filled with wonder. At last we feel

that the seed we have planted and tended will come to fruitfulness in the fullness of time.

SUNDAY, NOVEMBER 6

We plowed through the first sleet storm of the winter to get to the Fairhaven service this morning. But there was a good congregation despite the muddy roads.

As soon as Ed stepped into the church, Ken Webster approached him. "May I have a word during the service?" he asked, and he waved a slip of paper before Ed's eyes. It was a check from a co-operative shipping company for twenty-one dollars.

"From the sale of the first church calf. Course it's Mr. Stanton's," he said triumphantly.

After church there was much discussion over the announcement. No one was more interested than little Louise.

"How's the big fat hen coming?" I asked her.

"She isn't so fat yet, but I've got a customer," she said. She hesitated. "I've been thinking, if I just let her lay a few more eggs before I sell her to Grandma . . ."

"You'll have a few more nickels for the church debt?"

She nodded.

SATURDAY, NOVEMBER 12

This past week has been an exhausting nightmare. Ed has been sick. He ran a high temperature all week and had the aches and pains of a severe attack of the flu. I felt like a pretty helpless little woman. We had our first wave of winter during my furnace stoking days. How I grew to dread those endless trips up and down the rickety cellar steps!

The preacher is feeling better now. It seems good to have

119

him firing the furnace and worrying about the antifreeze in the car radiator.

And today has been as different from those just passed as the scarlet sumac from the brown, withered grass. Ernie Mills stopped in this morning. He'd just heard that Ed was sick. "Anything you could use a man for?" he asked in a cheery voice. Just when the woodpile, except for the heavy pieces, was exhausted! I sent him to the woodshed, and he surely did his duty by us.

Then he came in and entertained Ed with stories of the rough-and-ready life on the north border.

"Man, you need a rest," he said when he arose to go. "Can't you get away fer a while?"

"Maybe we will," Ed answered and then thanked him for his thoughtfulness.

"Gebby," he said, grasping Ed's hand, "it's mighty little I've done to repay your goodness." Then half to himself he added, "Man, I dread to think of what me an' my family would've gone through if the church hadn't found us—and cared."

FRIDAY, NOVEMBER 18

As we drove home after our week in the city, we felt the season's change in the air. Even the golds and russets of autumn are gone now, and a smoky haze has settled over the stubble fields and corn shocks. We feel grateful indeed for our rural parish, for the humble little churches and the friendly people we serve. We are grateful, too, that this year on our country circuit has opened the door for many years of fruitful, rewarding life. The kind, cool country has taken us back to its heart—and we don't have to discuss the reality of God to sense His continuing companionship.

We went immediately over to the Gorman church. The neat white tower stood out against the long, slanting rays of the afternoon sun. While we were gone last week, the new furnace was installed, the deep red carpet was laid down the center aisle of the church, and the rolling door between the new and old portions of the building was put in. But we were most eager to see the completed memorial window.

We stepped from the entranceway into the quiet little sanctuary. The rose and purple hues in the large east window blessed the atmosphere with warmth and subdued light. Automatically I walked up the aisle to the front, where my cello was still sitting since last Sunday's service. I picked it up and began playing. "Ave Maria" and the Bach "Arioso" sang from my instrument. As I played, I studied the varied colors in the window. I thought of the gentle old friends who had placed it there, of the rich, warm colors in their familiar gardenful of flowers, of the sun setting in rosy wonder behind the simple church they loved. Ed sauntered to the back of the church and fingered the neat bronze inscription beneath the window:

To the Glory of God
Who Made Seedtime and Harvest

in loving memory of
Ralph A. Gunter

WITHDRAWN
from
Funderburg Library

R61
G264

To

The Rural Parishes We Have Served

WHERE WE HAVE PLANTED WITH CARE

WATCHED WITH PATIENCE AND

HARVESTED WITH GRATITUDE

LIBRARY

42913

MANCHESTER COLLEGE